D1083454

Structure Drill through

1. Structure Drill in

G W O Y E U   M O F A N N   J I U H F A A   L I A N N S H Y I

1959

Speech Patterns edited by **B. Schindler,** Dr.Phil.
and **W. Simon,** Dr.Phil., D.Lit., F.B.A.

Chinese

National Language . Gwoyeu

First Fifty Patterns by **W. Simon,** Dr.Phil., D.Lit., F.B.A., Professor of Chinese in the University of London

and **T. C. Chao,** LL.B., sometime Lecturer in Chinese at the School of Oriental Studies, University of London

Percy Lund, Humphries & Co. Ltd · 12 Bedford Square, London WC1

First Edition 1945
Second Revised Edition 1959

Printed in Great Britain by Percy Lund, Humphries & Co Ltd

Foreword

The Series 'Structure Drill through Speech Patterns' is offered to Teachers and Students as a new tool for teaching and learning languages. Each volume of **Structure Drill** consists of fifty Speech Patterns, dealing with one structural feature at a time. It is intended to publish more than one volume for each language so that Speech Patterns devoted to any one language will include all important syntactical features and may eventually be used as a refresher course for the whole of its syntax. Furthermore, special consideration will be given to **Idioms** in the more advanced volumes of any one language.

As indicated by the title, the objective of the new Series is to **drill** the student in, not merely to acquaint him with, the correct usage of certain structural features. For this reason, as many as fifteen sentences are normally given to illustrate each Speech Pattern, and it will be observed that all the sentences represent **actual speech.** Once the first sentence of a pattern has been explained to the student, he may be expected to deal satisfactorily with the other sentences since his difficulties are then limited to Vocabulary and Idiom. The student therefore must never be allowed to look at the solution before having attempted a rendering of his own. (The same procedure should be adopted if the student teaches himself.)

After a Speech Pattern has been worked through, all its sentences should be read aloud several times either by individual students or in chorus to ensure their full assimilation. As most Speech Patterns consist of two parts, the recurrent 'headings' and their 'complements', certain **anticipations** as to what is to follow are bound to arise in the student's mind, once the heading is said or read out, and it may be noted that the understanding of foreign languages without any special effort depends to a great extent—as does, in fact, the understanding of our mother tongue—on such anticipations being automatic.

For many Speech Patterns alternative headings or complements have been indicated. Both teachers and students may like to think out further alternatives on their own. The Speech Patterns have been arranged alphabetically according to the English heading, but a systematic survey of all structural features and an alphabetical index of the headings in each foreign language have also been included. The alphabetical arrangement according to the English heading will help teachers and students to find their bearings in the book easily. As opposed to any systematic arrangement, it also leaves the student without any clue as to which pattern may be chosen next by his teacher, and, as explained above it is essential that the sentences should be translated as **unseens.** Furthermore the alphabetical arrangement will facilitate a comparative study of the rendering of any one Speech Pattern into several or all the languages included in the Series.

In conclusion. the Editors wish to express the hope that this new approach to the study of languages may prove stimulative and effective.

B. Schindler
W. Simon

London: 1 August 1945

PREFACE TO THE FIRST EDITION

The Chinese Speech Patterns (in National Language—Gwoyeu) are the first to be published in the new Series **Structure Drill.** They are also novel in so far as they are written down only in the new Official Chinese Latin Script (Gwoyeu Romatzyh), though a certain number of Chinese characters have been added in the Notes. Students may like to turn the whole of the Chinese sentences into Chinese script. This exercise will also prove very helpful for assimilating both patterns and illustrative sentences.

Some kind of apology is perhaps due for the short titles given to each Speech Pattern. It was felt, however, that teachers and students might prefer these titles to the number or the necessarily incomplete 'heading' when referring to a Pattern from memory.

While the undersigned is responsible for the choice of the patterns and their sentences, final responsibility for the Chinese wording lies in each single case with Mr. **T. C. Chao,** LL.B., Lecturer in Chinese at the School of Oriental Studies, University of London. Mr. **Chao** also wrote the Chinese characters in the Notes.

W. Simon

Twickenham: 1 August 1945

PREFACE TO THE SECOND EDITION

This revised edition has benefited greatly from various corrections offered by colleagues and former students. Special thanks are due to Professor L. S. Yang of Harvard University, who kindly read through the whole of the Chinese text and made a number of very valuable suggestions.

W. Simon

9 March 1958

Table of Contents

English Index

Chinese Index

Grammatical Index

Structure Drill	Jiuhfaa Liannshyi

Patterns I—L

I THE GOOD BOY

After he had . . .

1 finished his home-work, he went to bed at once

2 received a letter from his mother, he answered it immediately

3 put out the light, he fell asleep at once

4 taken his medicine, he felt much better

5 read one page of the love story, he did not read on

6 finished the book, he returned it at once to the library

7 attended his classes, he went home immediately

8 taken his holidays he worked even harder

9 had been punished he repented his evil deeds

10 drawn the first prize he shared the money with all his relatives and friends

11 read the biography of a great man he followed his example

12 failed in the examination he registered at once to take it again

13 received an invoice he sent his cheque by return

14 fallen in love he at once proposed to the lady

15 taken a wife he lived happily ever after

Alternative Headings and/or **Complements**: Cp. Pattern V (*As soon as . . .*).

Ta . . . yiihow . . .

1 **Ta** baa gongkeh yuhbeywanle **yiihow** lihkeh jiow shueyjiaw-chiuhle

2 **Ta** jiedawle ta muuchin-de yihfeng shinn **yiihow** gaanjiin jiow shiee hweishinn le

3 **Ta** baa deng miehle **yiihow** lihkeh jiow shueyjaurle

4 **Ta** chyle yaw **yiihow** jiow jyueder hao-duo le

5 **Ta** kannle jehgeh liann-ay[1]-de guhshyh yiyeh **yiihow** jiow bwu tzay wanq shiah kann le

6 **Ta** kannwanle shu **yiihow** lihkeh jiow baa ta jihhwei twushugoan[2] chiuhle

7 **Ta** shanq keh **yiihow** lihkeh hwei jia le

8 **Ta** guohle jiahch(y)i **yiihow** jiow gongtzuoh genq chyn le

9 **Ta** bey cherngfarle[3] **yiihow** jiow howhoei[4] tade tsuoll le

10 **Ta** derle tourtsae[5] **yiihow** jiow baa chyan fen geei tade yichieh chinchi-perngyeoumen le

11 **Ta** dwule yigeh yeou ming-de ren de juann[6] **yiihow** jiow faangshiaw[7] jehgeh ren

12 **Ta** kaoshyh buh jyi ger[8] le **yiihow** lihkeh jiow baw ming tzay kao le

13 **Ta** jiedawle fapiaw **yiihow** lihkeh jiow sonq tade jypiaw[9] chiuh le

14 **Ta** ay *ta* le **yiihow** jiow lihkeh shianq *ta* chyou huen[10] le

15 **Ta** cheule shyifull **yiihow** yeongyeuan jiow heen kuayleh le

---

Notes: 1 戀愛 2 圖書館 3 懲罰 4 後悔 5 頭彩

6 傳 7 倣傚 8 及格 9 支票 10 求婚

II CONTRARY TO EXPECTATION

Although . . .

1 the light was on he went to sleep
2 the house was unfurnished the rent was very high
3 he was paid a high salary he did not want to stay (in the job)
4 his parents spent a great deal of money on his education his behaviour is not that of an educated person
5 he had been run over by a car he was only slightly injured
6 the police station was next door our house was burgled
7 the dictionary is cheap it is very good and very reliable
8 he had little money he never came without bringing us a present
9 I had the fire on all day I could not get the room warm
10 he was a rich man he was very unhappy
11 he was very fond of children he never married
12 the beginning of this novel is interesting it soon becomes very dull
13 the crisis is over the political situation is still rather tense
14 the best doctors attended him he died a few days after he had gone to hospital
15 the manuscript is incomplete it is very valuable

Alternative Headings and/or **Complements**:

II

Sweiran . . . dannsh . . .

1 **Sweiran** deng kaij **dannsh** ta shueyjaurle

2 **Sweiran** farngtz-liibian meiyeou jiajiuh, **dannsh** farngtzu heen dah

3 **Sweiran** tade gongchyan heen dah, **dannsh** ta buh keen daij[1] [*also:* tzay tzuoh jehjiann shyh]

4 **Sweiran** tade fuhmuu huale heen duo-de chyan jiawyuh ta **dannsh** tade tayduh bwu shianq sh showguoh jiawyuh-de

5 **Sweiran** ta bey [*also:* jiaw] chihche penqle, **dannsh** ta show-de shang heen ching

6 **Sweiran** jiingcharjyu[2] sh woomende jiehbiiel[3], **dannsh** tzeir jinn woomende farngtz laile

7 **Sweiran** heen pyanyih, **dannsh** jehbeen tzyhdean sh heen hao heen keekaw

8 **Sweiran** tade chyan heen shao, **dannsh** ta lai-de shyrhow tzoong day yijiann liiwuh

9 **Sweiran** woode huoo shaule yihtian, **dannsh** woo mei fal baa utz shau noan (·huo)

10 **Sweiran** ta sh yigeh kuohren,[4] **dannsh** ta heen bwu kuayleh

11 **Sweiran** ta heen shiihuan (sheau) hairtzmen, **dannsh** ta tzoongbu cheu shyifull

12 **Sweiran** jehgeh sheaushuo-de chiitour heen yeou chiuhwey, **dannsh** heen kuay-de jiow biann heen gantzaw[5] le

13 **Sweiran** jehgeh weishean guohchiuhle, **dannsh** jenqjyh-chyngshyng[6] hairsh heen jiinjang[7]

14 **Sweiran** tzueyhao-de dayfu jyh ta, **dannsh** ta daw iyuann jiitian yiihow jiow syyle

15 **Sweiran** jehgeh shieebeen sh buh chyuan, **dannsh** ta sh heen yeou jiahjyr

---

Notes: [1] 待着 [2] 警察局 [3] 隔壁儿 [4] 闊人

[5] 乾燥 [6] 政治情形 [7] 緊張

III SHAM

. . . **as if** . . .

1 This House looks **as if** it is going to collapse at any moment

2 The Headmaster looked **as if** this matter did not concern him at all

3 She looked **as if** she was going to cry at any moment

4 He (his face) was very pale **as if** he was going to faint at any moment

5 My father looked at me **as if** he had never seen me before

6 My mother looked **as if** she was very ill

7 It looks **as if** it is going to rain

8 They looked at him **as if** he was drunk.

9 He cried **as if** he was never to see us again

10 He works **as if** he were going to take the examination to-morrow

11 The shirts which have come back from the laundry look **as if** they have not been washed at all

12 This picture looks **as if** it were genuine, but it is only a very good copy

---

Alternative Headings and/or **Complements:**

III

. . . haoshianq . . .

1 Jehsuoo farngtz kannj **haoshianq** lihkeh jiow yaw tale[1]

2 Shiawjaang kannj **haoshianq** jehjiann shyhchyng dueyyu ta yihdeal meiyeou guanshih

3 *Ta* kannj **haoshianq** lihkeh jiow yaw kule

4 Tade lean heen bair **haoshianq** lihkeh jiow yaw iundaole

5 Woo fuhchin [*also:* Jiafuh, Jiayan[2]] kann woo **haoshianq** yiichyan meiyeou kannjiannguoh woo (-de yanqtz)

6 Woo muuchin [*also:* Jiamuu] kannj **haoshianq** binq-de heen lihhay

7 Tian kannj **haoshianq** kuay yaw shiah yeu le [*also:* kuay yaw shiah yeu-de yanqtz]

8 Tamen kann ta **haoshianq** ta he tzueyle (-de yanqtz)

9 Ta kule **haoshianq** ta yeongyeuan bwu yaw tzay jiann woomen (-de yanqtz) le

10 Ta tzuoh gongkeh **haoshianq** mingtian jiow yaw kaoshyh le

11 Nahshie tsorng shii-i-farng hweilai-de hannshan kannj **haoshianq** sh yihdeal meiyeou shii(guoh)-de

12 Jehjang huall kannj **haoshianq** sh jen-de, dann bwuguoh sh yihjang heen hao-de jea-de

---

Note:

IV LIFE INSURANCE

As long as . . .

1 I live you have nothing to fear

2 I know about it, I don't mind where you go or at what time you come back

3 this man does not cause any trouble, there is no reason why I should interfere

4 he does his work properly, I do not bother about his political activities

5 we get there in time, I do not mind whether we walk, go by car or by train

6 we are always prepared to face the danger when it comes, I see no reason at present why we should not enjoy ourselves

7 he expresses his political views properly I do not mind whether they are liberal or conservative

8 we all keep together there is no harm (difficulty) in our having different opinions on various matters

9 I have this position, our firm cannot dismiss her

10 this principle is adhered to, we shall never find a permanent solution of this problem

---

Alternative Headings and/or **Complements:** For sentences with 'or' cp. Pattern XXXIII.

IV

Jyyyaw . . .

1 woo hwoj, meiyeou nii kee pah-de shyhchyng

2 woo jydaw, woo buh goan nii daw sherme dihfang chiuh huohsh sherme shyrhow hweilai

3 jehgeh ren buh yiinchii[1] mafarn[2] lai, meiyeou woo gansheh[3] ta-de liiyou[4]

4 ta tzuoh shyh tzuoh-de maanyih, woo buh goan tade jenqjyh-hwodonq[5] tzeeme yanq

5 woomen nenggow joen shyrhow daw nahlii, woo buh goan tzoouj huohsh tzuoh chihche huohsh tzuoh huooche chiuh

6 weishean[6] lai-de shyrhow woomen yeongyeuan yeou yuhbey, jiuh woo kann shianntzay meiyeou woomen bwu kuayleh-de liiyou[4]

7 ta baa tade jenqjyh-yihjiann heen jenqdanq-de fabeauchulai, woo buh goan nah yihjiann sh tzyhyou-de huohsh baoshoou-de

8 woomen neng twanjye[7], sweiran dueyyu joongx shyhchyng yeou buhtorng-de yihjiann dann meiyeou sherme kuennnan

9 woo yeou jehgen dihwey, woomen gongsy buh neng baa *ta* cheh jyr[8]

10 woomen baoshoou jehgeh dawlii[9], dueyyu jehgeh wenntyi woomen jiow jaobudaw yigeh yeongjeou-de jieejyue[10]

Notes: [1] 引起來 [2] 麻煩 [3] 干涉 [4] 理由 [5] 活動 [6] 危險 [7] 團結 [8] 撤職 [9] 道理 [10] 解決

V IMMEDIATE ACTION

As soon as . . .

1 he saw me he got up from his chair and welcomed me very cordially

2 it stopped raining we set out on our journey

3 my father entered the room she left immediately

4 I received this news I sent a telegram to his mother

5 the house was ready we moved in

6 the dog started barking the thieves ran away

7 he had finished his speech everybody applauded wildly

8 he had sold his property he left the country

9 the fire goes (went) out the room is (was) cold [*or:* the sun sets it gets cold]

10 the ship struck the mine it sank

11 you give him money he will buy books

12 the doctor arrived he felt immediately much better

13 he has recovered he will go to the south

14 he had missed two or three lessons he was unable to catch up

15 he starts speaking you realise that he is a foreigner

Alternative Headings and/or **Complements**: Cp. Pattern I (*After he had . . .*).

V

. . . yih (yi) . . . jiow . . .

1 Ta **yi** kannjiann woo, **jiow** tsorng tade yiitz-shanq jannchiilaile heen rehlieh[1]-de huan-yng woo

2 **Yih** tyngjyy shiah yeu, woomen **jiow** chii shen le

3 Woo fuhchin **yi** jinn daw utz-lii lai, *ta* **jiow** lihkeh tzooule

4 Woo **yih** jiedaw jehgeh shiaushyi, **jiow** geei tade muuchin daale yigeh diannbaw

5 Farngtz **yih** hao, woomen **jiow** banjinnlaile [*also:* banjinnchiuhle]

6 Goou **yih** yeauchiilai, tzeir **jiow** paole

7 Ta **yih** jeangwanle, dahjia **jiow** jyilih-de guu jaang

8 Ta **yi** mayle tade chaanyeh, **jiow** likai gwo le

9 Huoo **yi** mieh, utz **jiow** leengle [*or:* Tayyang **yi** law, **jiow** leeng le]

10 Chwan **yi** jonq[2] shoeilei[3], ta **jiow** chernshiahchiuhle

11 Nii **yih** geei ta chyan, ta **jiow** yaw mae shu

12 Dayfu **yi** daw, ta **jiow** lihkeh jyueder hao-duo le

13 Ta **yi** fuhyuan, **jiow** yaw wanq nanbian chiuh

14 Ta **yi** lah leangsan keh, **jiow** gaanbushanq le

15 Ta **yih** shuochii huah lai, nii **jiow** keeyii jydaw ta sh waygworen

---

Notes:

1 

2 中

3 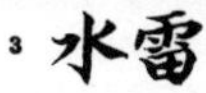

VI PRELIMINARIES

Before I . . . I usually . . .

1 **Before I** go to bed **I usually** drink a cup of tea

2 **Before I** give my lecture **I usually** smoke a cigarette

3 **Before I** write a paper **I usually** consult a bibliography (list of reference books) on the subject

4 **Before I** put a letter in the envelope **I usually** look the letter over again

5 **Before I** cross a road **I usually** look left and right

6 **Before I** go down to dinner **I usually** have a quarter of an hour's rest

7 **Before I** read a book **I usually** look at the preface and the table of contents

8 **Before I** go on a journey **I usually** make a list of the things which I am likely to forget

9 **Before I** make an appointment **I usually** look at my diary

10 **Before I** make an important decision **I usually** think the matter over for a day or two

11 **Before I** start my work in the afternoon **I usually** go for a stroll for ten minutes

12 **Before I** go out **I usually** make sure that the lights are switched off

---

Alternative Headings and/or **Complements**: Cp. Pattern L (*Why did you go without . . .?*).

VI

Woo tzay (mei) . . . yiichyan, jawlih . . .

1 **Woo tzay** (**mei**) shueyjiaw **yiichyan, jawlih** he yihwoan char

2 **Woo tzay** (**mei**) jeangyean **yiichyan, jawlih** chou yihjy ian

3 **Woo tzay** (**mei**) shiee yipiann wenjang **yiichyan, jawlih** kann-iv guanyu jehgeh tyimuh-de tsankaoshu-dantz[1]

4 **Woc tzay** (**mei**) baa shinn ge tzay shinnfeng-lii **yiichyan, jawlih** tzay kann yibiann

5 **Woo tzay** (**mei**) guoh jie **yiichyan, jawlih** wanq tzuoobial yowbial kann yitsyh

6 **Woo tzay** (**mei**) shiahchiuh chy woanfann **yiichyan, jawlih** shioushyi yikeh jong

7 **Woo tzay** (**mei**) kann yihbeen shu **yiichyan, jawlih** kannx shiuh[2] her muhluh[3]

8 **Woo tzay** (**mei**) chii shen **yiichyan, jawlih** baa woo heen rongyih wanq-de dongshi jih tzay yigeh dantz-shanq

9 **Woo tzay** (**mei**) dinq iuehuey **yiichyan, jawlih** kann-iv woode ryhjihbeel[4]

10 **Woo tzay** (**mei**) jyuedinq yijiann yawjiin-de shyh **yiichyan, jawlih** jenjwo yihleang tian

11 **Woo tzay** (**mei**) kaishyy shiahwuu-de gongtzuoh **yiichyan, jawlih** lioudar[5] shyrfen jong-de gongfu

12 **Woo tzay** (**mei**) chu mel **yiichyan, jawlih** kann-iv dianndeng chyuan guanle meiyeou

---

Notes: [1] 參考書單子 [2] 序 [3] 目錄

[4] 日記本兒 [5] 遛達

VII VOTE OF THANKS

But for him, I should have . . .

1 been dismissed

2 failed in the examination

3 never come back to London

4 not have been able to go on

5 had nobody to consult with

6 missed the train

7 left the meeting [*or:* political party] long ago

8 read as many novels as I liked

9 written a very rude letter

10 taken my holiday next week

11 been without support [*or:* money]

12 gone with you to the cinema

13 been unable to write this book

14 started a fight right away

15 gone to prison

Alternative Headings and/or **Complements:** Cp. Patterns XV (*He almost . . .*) and XXIX (*If you are not careful*). For sentence **8** cp. also XXXI, sentences **2** and **4**

VII

Yaw bwush ta, woo jiow . . .

1 bey cheh jyr[1] le

2 kao buh jyi ger[2] le

3 tzoongbu [*also:* laobu] hwei daw Luenduen laile

4 buh neng tzay wanqshiah tzuoh le

5 meiyeou ren kee wennle [*also:* wenn-iv le]

6 wuh[3] che le

7 tzao likai jehgeh huey [*or:* jenqdaang] le

8 niannle woo shiihuan niann-de nahmeshie been sheaushuo le

9 shieele heen bwu-kehchih-de yihfeng shinn le

10 shiahshingchyi [*also:* shiahliibay] shioushyi le

11 meiyeou ren bang woo mang [*or:* geei woo chyan] le

12 torng nii kann diannyiing chiuhle

13 buh neng shiee jehbeen shu le

14 lihkeh daa jiah le

15 daw lau[4]-lii chiuhle

Notes: [1] 撤職 [2] See p. 3, n. 8. [3] 悮 [4] 牢

Note the perfective particle *le* at the end of all the sentences.

VIII INQUISITIVE

Did you . . . or . . . ?

1 **Did you** eat one piece [*or:* slice] of cake **or** two?

2 **Did you** take two pieces of sugar **or** three?

3 **Did you** buy one hat **or** two?

4 **Did you** order two pairs of gloves **or** three?

5 **Did you** give him ten dollars **or** twenty?

6 **Did you** order five dishes **or** six?

7 **Did you** want one hundred sheets of paper **or** two hundred?

8 **Did you** repair one shoe **or** two?

9 **Did you** rent four rooms **or** five?

10 **Did you** add five drops of the medicine **or** eight?

11 **Did you** order one suit of clothes [*or:* one pair of trousers] **or** two?

12 **Did you** hire one rickshaw [*or:* pedicab] **or** two?

13 **Did you** plant one cherry-tree and two apple-trees **or** two cherry-trees and one apple-tree?

14 **Did you** hire five donkeys **or** eight?

15 **Did you** borrow four books from him **or** five?

Alternative Headings and/or **Complements:** More examples can easily be made by changing the objects and their classifiers. Cp. Patterns XVI and XXXIII.

VIII

Nii . . . (ne) hairsh . . . (ne)?

1 **Nii** chyle yikuay [*or:* yipiann] jidanngau (**ne**) **hairsh** leangkuay [*or* leangpiann] (**ne**)?

2 **Nii** nale leangkuay tarng (**ne**) **hairsh** sankuay (**ne**)?

3 **Nii** maele yihdiing mawtz (**ne**) **hairsh** leangdiing (**ne**)?

4 **Nii** dinqle leangfuh[1] shooutawl (**ne**) **hairsh** sanfuh (**ne**)?

5 **Nii** geeile ta shyrkuay chyan (**ne**) **hairsh** ellshyrkuay (**ne**)?

6 **Nii** dinqle wuugeh tsay (**ne**) **hairsh** liowgeh (**ne**)?

7 **Nii** yawle yihbae-jang jyy (**ne**) **hairsh** ellbae jang (**ne**)?

8 **Nii** shiouhaole [*also:* shiouliile] yihjy shye (**ne**) **hairsh** leangjy (**ne**)?

9 **Nii** tzule syhjian utz (**ne**) **hairsh** wuujian (**ne**)?

10 **Nii** jia(shanq)le wuudi yaw (**ne**) **hairsh** badi (**ne**)?

11 **Nii** dinqle yitaw [*also:* yihshen] ifwu [*or:* yihtyau kuhtz] (**ne**) **hairsh** leangtaw [*also:* leangshen] [*or:* leangtyau] (**ne**)?

12 **Nii** guhle yiliang yangche [*or:* sanluelche] (**ne**) **hairsh** lianghanq (**ne**)?

13 **Nii** jonqle yihke ingtaurshuh, leangke pyngguooshuh (**ne**) **hairsh** leangke ingtaurshuh, yihke pyngguooshuh (**ne**)?

14 **Nii** guhle wuutour liu (**ne**) **hairsh** batour (**ne**)?

15 **Nii** shianq ta jiehle syhbeen shu (**ne**) **hairsh** wuubeen (**ne**)?

Note: 

IX HARD TO BELIEVE

Do you mean to say that . . .

1 you don't love me any more?

2 you still have not written that letter [*or:* sent this parcel]?

3 he left without saying good-bye?

4 you are not going to help me?

5 he has again offered his resignation?

6 you have never heard from him again?

7 he has gone bankrupt [*or:* stole the money]?

8 you do not know the latest news?

9 she is asking for a divorce?

10 he told me a lie?

11 he cannot afford to buy a car?

12 he committed suicide [*or:* was poisoned]?

13 her illness is incurable [*or:* her case is hopeless]?

14 he is insane?

15 I shall never see her again?

Alternative Headings and/or **Complements**:

Nandaw . . . ma?

1 **Nandaw** nii bwu ay woo le **ma?**

2 **Nandaw** nii hair mei(yeou) shiee nahfeng shinn [*or:* sonq jehgeh bauguoo] **ma?**

3 **Nandaw** ta mei(yeou) shuo tzayjiann jiow tzooule **ma?**

4 **Nandaw** nii bwu yuannyih bang woo mang **ma?**

5 **Nandaw** ta yow yaw tsyr jyr le **ma?**

6 **Nandaw** nii tzoong mei tzay jiedaw tade shiaushyi **ma?**

7 **Nandaw** ta poh chaan[1] le [*or:* toule jeh chyan le] **ma?**

8 **Nandaw** nii buh jydaw tzueyshin-de shiaushyi **ma?**

9 **Nandaw** *ta* yaw li huen[2] **ma?**

10 **Nandaw** ta gen woo sa [*also:* shuo] hoang[3] le **ma?**

11 **Nandaw** ta maebuchii yilianq chihche **ma?**

12 **Nandaw** ta tzyh shale [*or:* bey dwusyyle] **ma?**

13 **Nandaw** *ta* jehgeh binq jyhbuleau [*or:* *ta* meiyeou shiwanq le] **ma?**

14 **Nandaw** ta feng le **ma?**

15 **Nandaw** woo yeongyeuan buh neng tzay jiann *ta* le **ma?**

Notes: [1] 破產 [2] 離婚 [3] 撒謊

X DISCRIMINATION

Don't forget this is not . . .

1 my fountain-pen
2 his india-rubber
3 her own dog
4 an encyclopedia
5 a beginners' class
6 an advanced class
7 an infectious disease
8 a novel
9 a short story
10 a Ph.D. thesis
11 a student's essay
12 a primer

13 a true story
14 his real name
15 an examination
16 a formal meeting
17 the letter he showed you when he had just arrived
18 what he promised you a month ago
19 the book given to him by your grandfather
20 a very polite [*or:* satisfactory] reply

21 a question that anybody can answer
22 a matter that interests him very much
23 a matter that we can discuss when he is there

Alternative Headings and/or **Complements:** Cp. Patterns XLII and XLIII. Use sentence 12 of Pattern III as a model to modify the Pattern into '*Don't forget this is only*'.

X

Bwuyaw [*also:* Bye] wanqjih jeh bwu sh . . .

1 woode tzyhlaishoeibii

2 tade shianqpyi

3 *ta* tzyhjii-de goou

4 yihbeen baekechyuanshu[1]

5 yigeh chujyiban

6 yigeh gaujyiban

7 yihjoong chwanraanbinq

8 yigeh sheaushuo

9 yigeh doanpian-sheaushuo

10 yigeh borshyh-luennwen

11 yipiann shyuesheng-de wenjang

12 yihbeen jiawkeshu

13 yigeh jen-de guhshyh

14 tade jen shinq

15 (yigeh) kaoshyh

16 yigeh jenqshyh[2]-de huey

17 ta gang daw-de shyrhow ta geei nii kann-de nahfeng shinn

18 yigeh yueh-yiichyan ta yinqsheu [*also:* ingsheu] nii-de nahjiann shyh

19 nii tzuufuh sonqgeei ta-de nahbeen shu

20 yigeh heen kehchih-de [*or:* heen maanyih-de] hweidar [*also:* hweishinn]

21 wuluenn sherme ren du neng dar-de wenntyi

22 dueyyu ta heen yeou chiuhwey-de yijiann shyh

23 ta tzay jehlii-de shyrhow woomen neng taoluenn-de wenntyi

Notes: [1] 百科全書 [2] 正式

XI REGARDLESS OF COSTS

Even if . . .

1 we have to spend another 100,000 dollars we shall get this work [*or:* bridge, building] completed

2 he does survive the operation he will always be a sick man

3 you succeed in speaking to his secretary he himself will never wish to see you

4 nobody likes him I shall never abandon him

5 you had been able to catch the train you would still have been half an hour late

6 he was justified in his criticism he should not have used such bad language

7 this war comes to a speedy end we shall have to face great difficulties in the future

8 he passes the examination he will never do for this job [*or:* be suitable for this post]

9 the experts do not approve of this project I feel that a few words from a layman may perhaps be of some use

10 we get a few musicians together we shall never be able to form a band

---

Alternative Headings and/or **Complements**: Cp. Pattern XXXI (*In any case . . .*)

XI

Jyibiann . . . yee

1 woomen bihdeei tzay hua shyrwann-kuay chyan [*also:* shyrwann yuan] woomen **yee** baa jehgeh gongtzuoh [*or:* jehtyau chyau, jehtzuoh lou] wancherng

2 jingguoh jehtsyh shooushuh ta hair neng hwoj, ta **yee** yeong-yeuan sh yigeh binqren le

3 nii nenggow her tade shujih shuo huah, ta **yee** buhkeen tzyhjii jiann nii

4 meiyeou ren shiihuan ta, woo **yee** tzoongbu [*also:* laobu, yeongyeuanbu] likai ta

5 nii neng gaanshanq che nii **yee** woanle banngeh jongtou le

6 tade pipyng sh heen gongpyng, ta **yee** buh inggai shuo nahme huay-de huah

7 jehtsyh [*also:* jehgeh] jannjeng kuay daawanle, woomen jianglai **yee** yaw yuhjiann heen dah-de kuennnan

8 ta kaoshyh jyi ger[1] le [*or:* tade kaoshyh cherng gong le], ta **yee** buh neng tzuoh jehjiann shyh [*or:* ta yee dueyyu jehgeh dihwey buh shiangyi]

9 juanjia bwu tzanncherng jehgeh jihhuah, woo jyueder yigeh wayharng-de ren jiijiuh huah yeesheu **yee** yeou yonqchuh

10 woomen nenggow jaodaw jiigeh inyuehjia, woomen tzoong **yee** tzuubucherng yigeh inyuehduey

---

Note: [1] See p. 3, n. 8

XII COUÉISM

. . . every day

1 The weather is now getting better . . .

2 His Chinese [*or:* English, French, German, Russian] becomes more fluent . . .

3 He gets stronger . . .

4 His pronunciation [*or:* intonation] becomes better (clearer) . . .

5 Our airplanes become faster . . .

6 This district becomes bigger . . .

7 His temper gets more violent . . .

8 His knowledge increases . . .

9 He earns more money . . .

10 His behaviour gets worse . . .

11 Our coal gets less . . .

12 The days now are longer . . .

13 Food becomes scarcer . . .

14 Science is advancing . . .

15 This party becomes more influential . . .

Alternative Headings and/or **Complements**: Cp. Pattern XIX (*His . . . than mine*)

XII

. . . yihtian bii yihtian . . .

1 Tianchih shianntzay **yihtian bii yihtian** hao

2 Tade Jongwen [*or:* Ingwen, Fahwen, Derwen, Ehwen] **yihtian bii yihtian** lioulih[1]

3 Ta **yihtian bii yihtian** juanq

4 Tade koouin [*or:* chiangdiaw[2]] **yihtian bii yihtian** chingchuu

5 Woomende feiji **yihtian bii yihtian** kuay

6 Jey-i chiu **yihtian bii yihtian** dah

7 Tade pyichih **yihtian bii yihtian** lihhay

8 Tade jyshyh **yihtian bii yihtian** tzengjia

9 Ta juann-de chyan **yihtian bii yihtian** duo

10 Tade shyngwei[3] **yihtian bii yihtian** huay

11 Woomende mei **yihtian bii yihtian** shao

12 Shianntzay bairtian **yihtian bii yihtian** charng

13 Chy-de dongshi **yihtian bii yihtian** shao

14 Keshyue[4] **yihtian bii yihtian** jinnbuh

15 Jehgeh daang-de shyhlih [5] **yihtian bii yihtian** dah

Notes: [1] 流利 [2] 腔調 [3] 行為 [4] 科學
[5] 勢力

XIII ONCE BITTEN . . .

From now on (After that) I shall never . . . again

1 see him [*or:* write to him] **again**

2 believe **again** a word of what he says

3 set foot in this place **again**

4 **again** miss so good an opportunity

5 **again** ask him to do something for me

6 **again** say anything about my private affairs to him

7 invite him **again** into my house

8 be kind to him **again**

9 ask his advice **again**

10 **again** make any promises to him

11 take risks [*or:* gamble, smoke, drink] **again**

12 **again** pay any attention to him

13 contradict [*or:* criticize] him **again**

14 talk to him **again** without witnesses

15 **again** make an unprepared speech

Alternative Headings and/or **Complements:** Cp. Pattern XXXVI (*Next time don't . . .*)

XIII

Tsorng tsyy-yiihow woo yeongyeuan bwu tzay . . . le

1 jiann ta [*or:* geei ta shiee shinn] **le**[1]

2 shinn ta suoo shuo-de huah **le**

3 lai jehgeh dihfang **le**

4 shychiuh jehyanq hao-de [*or:* jehyanq-de hao] jihuey le

5 chiing ta tih woo tzuoh shyh **le**

6 gen ta shuo [*also:* tarn] syshyh le

7 chiing ta daw woode jia-lii lai **le**

8 day ta hao **le**

9 wenn tade yihjiann **le**

10 yinqsheu [*also:* ingsheu] ta le

11 maw shean [*or:* duu, chou ian, he jeou] **le**

12 juhyih [*also:* goan] ta **le**

13 faanbor [*or:* pipyng] ta **le**

14[2] **Tsorng tsyy-yiihow** meiyeou jenqren **woo yeongyeuan bwu tzay** her ta shuo huah **le**

15[2] **Tsorng tsyy-yiihow** meiyeou yuhbey **woo yeongyeuan bwu tzay** jeangyean **le**

Notes: [1] Note that the *le* at the end is indispensable (*buh . . . le* implying a break of continuity).

[2] Note the changed order of words which necessitated the repetition of the whole of the heading.

XIV LITTLE ERRANDS

Go to the . . . and fetch the . . .

1 **Go to the** kitchen **and fetch the** towel that is hanging on the wall

2 **Go to the** bedroom **and fetch the** little box on the table

3 **Go to the** study **and fetch the** Chinese dictionary that is on my writing-desk

4 **Go to the** garden **and fetch the** potatoes which are in the sack near the fence

5 **Go to the** laundry **and fetch the** washing that was sent there last week

6 **Go to the** class-room **and fetch the** two pieces of chalk that are in the book-case

7 **Go to the** bathroom **and fetch the** soap that is on the bath

8 **Go to the** hotel **and fetch the** case that father left there yesterday

9 **Go to the** Post Office **and fetch the** letters and parcels addressed to Mr. Lee

10 **Go to the** cellar **and fetch the** coal which is in the right hand corner

11 **Go to the** courtyard **and fetch the** hose which is lying near the wall

12 **Go to the** storeroom **and fetch the** bag of flour that is on the shelf

---

Alternative Headings and/or **Complements:**

XIV

Nii daw . . . chiuh baa . . . nalai

1 **Nii daw** chwufarng **chiuh baa** guah tzay chyang-shanq-de maujin **nalai**

2 **Nii daw** wohfarng(-lii) **chiuh baa** ge tzay juotz-shanq-de sheau herl **nalai**

3 **Nii daw** shufarng(-lii) **chiuh baa** ge tzay shieetzyhtair-shanq-de Jonggwo-tzyhdean **nalai**

4 **Nii daw** huayuan(-lii) **chiuh baa** kawjinn liba[1] koouday-lii-de shanyawdow[2] **nalai**

5 **Nii daw** shii-i-farng(-lii) **chiuh baa** shanqliibay sonqchiuh-de ishang **nalai**

6 **Nii daw** jiawshyh(-lii) **chiuh baa** shugueytz-lii-de leangkuay feenbii **nalai**

7 **Nii daw** shiitzaofarng(-lii) **chiuh baa** ge tzay shiitzaopern-shanq-de yitz **nalai**

8 **Nii daw** leugoan(-lii) **chiuh baa** fuhchin tzwotian liou-de shiangtz **nalai**

9 **Nii daw** youjenqjyu **chiuh baa** geei Lii Shg jihlai-de shinn her bauguoo du **nalai**

10 **Nii daw** dihyinntz[3](-lii) **chiuh baa** ge tzay yow jeau-shanq de mei **nalai**

11 **Nii daw** yuanntz(-lii) **chiuh baa** ge tzay chayang-parngbial de shoeilong[4] **nalai**

12 **Nii daw** huohjann[5](-lii) **chiuh baa** ge tzay jiahtz-shanq-de yih koouday miann **nalai**

Notes: [1] 籬笆 [2] 山藥豆 [3] 地窨子 [4] 水龍
[5] 貨棧

XV NARROW ESCAPE

He almost . . .

1 was drowned

2 missed the bus [*or:* train]

3 failed in the examination

4 broke his leg (*or:* arm)

5 burnt his fingers

6 lost his bet

7 ran over the dog

8 overslept

9 made a row

10 handed in his resignation

11 burst into tears

12 turned me out

13 found out about our secret

14 sued him for the money

15 escaped from prison

Alternative Headings and/or **Complements:** Cp. Patterns VII (*But for him . . .*) and XXIX (*If you are not careful . . .*).

XV

Ta chah yihdeal . . .

1 iansyyle

2 baa gonggonqchihche [*or:* huooche] wuhle

3 kao buh jyi ger[1] le

4 baa toei [*or:* gebey] shuaisherle[2]

5 baa shooujyr·tou shaule

6 daa duu daa shu le

7 baa goou yahsyyle[3]

8 chiiwoanle

9 daa jiah le

10 tsyr jyr[4] le

11 kuchiilaile

12 baa woo gaanchulaile

13 jydaw woomende mihmih[5] le

14 gaw ta hwan chyan le

15 tsorng jianlau-lii taurchulaile

Notes: [1] See p. 3, n. 8. [2] 折 [3] 軋死 Cp. p. 59, notes 1 and 2 [4] 辭職 [5] 祕密 *or* 秘密

XVI THE ECONOMIST

He did not even . . .

1 buy one book

2 write one letter

3 drink one cup of tea

4 say one word

5 spend one dollar [*or:* copper]

6 smoke one cigarette

7 take one day off

8 miss [*or:* attend] one class

9 eat one piece of cake

10 make one mistake

11 fire one shot

12 answer one question

13 break one plate

14 pick one flower

15 know one Chinese character

Alternative Headings and/or **Complements:** Cp. Pattern VIII (*Did you . . . or . . . ?*)

XVI

Ta lian . . . du [*also:* yee] mei(yeou) . . .

1 **Ta lian** yihbeen shu **du**[1] **mei(yeou)** mae

2 **Ta lian** yihfeng shinn **du mei(yeou)** shiee

3 **Ta lian** yihbei char **du mei(yeou)** he

4 **Ta lian** yijiuh huah **du mei(yeou)** shuo

5 **Ta lian** yikuay chyan [*or:* yigeh torngtzeel] **du mei(yeou)** hua

6 **Ta lian** yihjy ian **du mei(yeou)** chou

7 **Ta lian** yihtian jiah **du mei(yeou)** gaw

8 **Ta lian** yikeh **du mei(yeou)** lah[2] [*or:* shanq]

9 **Ta lian** yikuay jidanngau **du mei(yeou)** chy

10 **Ta lian** yigeh dihfang **du mei(yeou)** shuo tsuoh

11 **Ta lian** yihchiang[3] **du mei(yeou)** fanq

12 **Ta lian** yigeh wenntyi **du mei(yeou)** dar

13 **Ta lian** yigeh parntz **du mei(yeou)** daapoh

14 **Ta lian** yihduoo [*also:* yigeh] hual **du mei(yeou)** tsae

15 **Ta lian** yigeh Jonggwo tzyh **du mei(yeou)** rennshyh

Notes: [1] Note that instead of *du mei(yeou)* also *yee mei(yeou)* is possible.

[2]  [3] 

XVII AMNESIA

He had completely forgotten . . .

1 that he had made an appointment with his wife

2 that he had promised to repair my watch by to-day

3 that I had lent him fifty dollars

4 that he had met me before

5 that he was talking to a foreigner

6 that it was a holiday

7 that I intended to go abroad

8 where he left the book

9 where he had left off reading

10 to attend this important meeting

11 to phone me this morning

12 to set the alarm clock

13 to put a stamp on the letter

14 to put his bicycle in the shed

15 to listen to the news on the wireless

Alternative Headings: 'He did not remember in the least' (*Ta yihdeal yee bwu jihder*). 'How did you know . . .?' (*Nii tzeeme jydaw . . . ?*). **Alternative Complements:** 'to take his medicine' (*chy tade yaw*), 'to water the flowers' (*jiau hual*), 'to wind up the clock' (*baa jong shanqx*).

XVII

Ta wanchyuan wanqle . . .

1 ta her tade furen dinqle yigeh iuehuey le

2 ta yinqsheu [*also:* dayinq] jintian baa woode beau shiou hao le

3 woo jieh geei ta wuushyr kuay chyan le

4 ta yiichyan yuhjiannguoh [*also:* kannjiannguoh] woo le

5 ta her yigeh waygworen shuo huah le

6 nah-i tian (sh) fanq jiah le

7 woo daasuann chu gwo chiuh le

8 baa shu ge [*also:* liou] tzay naal [*also:* naalii] le

9 ta niann daw sherme dihfang le

10 tsanjia jehgeh yawjiin-de huey le

11 jintian tzaochern geei woo daa diannhuah la

12 baa nawjong[1] bohao[2] le

13 baa (yigeh) youpiaw tie tzay shinn-shanq le

14 baa tzyhshyngche ge tzay perngtz[3]-lii le

15 ting wushianndiann-de shinwen le

Notes: [1] 鬧鍾 [2] 撥好 [3] 棚子

XVIII IN EXILE

He has little opportunity to . . . there

1 talk English [*or:* Chinese, French, German, Russian] **there**

2 go to the theatre [*or:* cinema] **there**

3 see friends **there**

4 buy books **there**

5 read foreign newspapers **there**

6 consult an encyclopedia [*or:* reference books] **there**

7 talk to scholars **there**

8 have medical treatment **there**

9 attend lectures [*or:* attend classes] **there**

10 listen to the news on the wireless **there**

11 go for a stroll **there**

12 give a concert **there**

13 make use of his knowledge [*or:* experience] **there**

14 continue his research **there**

15 show talents **there**

Alternative Headings and/or **Complements:**

XVIII

Tzay nahlii ta . . . de jihuey heen shao

1 shuo Inggwo-huah [*or:* Jonggwo-huah, Fahgwo-huah, Dergwo-huah, Ehgwo-huah]-**de jihuey heen shao**

2 ting shih [*or:* kann diannyiing]-**de jihuey heen shao**

3 kann perngyeou-**de jihuey heen shao**

4 mae shu-**de jihuey heen shao**

5 kann waygwobaw-**de jihuey heen shao**

6 char baekechyuanshu [*or:* tsankaoshu[2]]-**de jihuey heen shao**

7 her niann shu-de ren tarn huah-**de jihuey heen shao**

8 bey isheng jyh-**de jihuey heen shao**

9 ting jeangyean [*or:* shanq keh]-**de jihuey heen shao**

10 ting wushianndiann shinwen-**de jihuey heen shao**

11 lioudar[3] [*also:* sann buh]-**de jihuey heen shao**

12 kai inyuehhuey-**de jihuey heen shao**

13 shyyyonq ta jyshyh [*or:* jingyann]-**de jihuey heen shao**

14 jihshiuh yanjiou-**de jihuey heen shao**

15 beaushyh tiantsair-**de jihuey heen shao**

Notes: [1] See p. 21, n. 1 [2] Cp. p. 13, n. 1 [3] See p. 13, n. 5.

XIX JEALOUS

His . . . than mine

1 **His** pencil is longer [*or:* much longer] **than mine**

2 **His** fountain-pen is thicker **than mine**

3 **His** clothes are better **than mine**

4 **His** watch is more expensive **than mine**

5 **His** children are more intelligent **than mine**

6 **His** wife is much prettier **than mine**

7 **His** salary is much higher **than mine**

8 **His** office hours are shorter **than mine**

9 **His** holidays are longer **than mine**

10 **His** health is better **than mine**

11 **His** office room is more elegant **than mine**

12 **His** boss is kinder **than mine**

13 **His** secretary is more reliable **than mine**

14 **His** typist is more efficient **than mine**

15 **His** mother-in-law died five years earlier **than mine**

Alternative Headings and/or **Complements:** Cp. Pattern XXXII (*In my opinion he is very . . .*).

XIX

Tade . . . bii woode . . .

1 **Tade** chianbii **bii woode** charng [*or:* charng-de duo]

2 **Tade** tzyhlaishoeibii **bii woode** tsu

3 **Tade** ishang **bii woode** hao

4 **Tade** beau **bii woode** guey

5 **Tade** hairtzmen **bii woode** tsongming

6 **Tade** furen **bii woode** haokann-de duo

7 **Tade** shinshoei **bii woode** dah-de duo

8 **Tade** bann gong shyrjian **bii woode** doan

9 **Tade** fanq jiah-de ryhtz **bii woode** duo

10 **Tade** shentii **bii woode** jiannkang

11 **Tade** gongshyhfarng **bii woode** kuoh

12 **Tade** jaangguan **bii woode** herchih

13 **Tade** mihshu **bii woode** genq keekaw [*also:* kawderjuh]

14 **Tade** daatzyhyuan **bii woode** genq yeou shiawliuh[1]

15 **Tade** yuehmuu **bii woode** tzao syyle wuunian

Note: [1] 效率

XX QUO VADIS?

I am going to . . .

1 town to do some shopping

2 the butcher to buy two pounds (catties) of beef

3 into the country to see friends

4 to the School [*or:* School of Oriental Studies] to learn Chinese

5 to the hairdresser to have my hair cut

6 to the cinema to see a film

7 to the theatre to see a play

8 to the kitchen to get a glass of water

9 to the bank to draw some [*or:* to pay in] money

10 to the China Society to attend a lecture

11 to the museum to see bronzes

12 to the library to read magazines

13 to the bus stop to catch a bus

14 to the station to meet a friend

15 to a jeweller's shop to buy a bracelet

Alternative Headings and/or **Complements:** I intend to . . . (*woo sheangyaw* . . .).

XX

Woo daw . . . chiuh

1 **Woo daw** cherng-lii mae dongshi **chiuh**

2 **Woo daw** rowpuh mae elljin niourow **chiuh**

3 **Woo daw** shiangshiah kann perngyeou **chiuh**

4 **Woo daw** Shyueshiaw [*or:* Dongfang-Wenhuah Shyueyuann[1]] shyue Jongwen **chiuh**

5 **Woo daw** liifaagoan lii faa **chiuh**

6 **Woo daw** diannyiingyuann kann diannyiing [*also:* yigeh piantz] **chiuh**

7 **Woo daw** shihyuann kann yihchu[2] shih **chiuh**

8 **Woo daw** chwufarng na yihbei shoei **chiuh**

9 **Woo daw** ynharng cheu [*or:* tswen] chyan **chiuh**

10 **Woo daw** Jonggwo Shyehuey[3] ting jeangyean **chiuh**

11 **Woo daw** borwuhyuann kann torngchih[4] **chiuh**

12 **Woo daw** twushugoan kann tzarjyh **chiuh**

13 **Woo daw** gonggonqchihchejann tzuoh gonggonqchihche **chiuh**

14 **Woo daw** huoochejann jie perngyeou **chiuh**

15 **Woo daw** jinjudiann mae yihjy jwotz[5] **chiuh**

Notes: [1] 東方文化學院 [2] 齣 [3] 協會

[4] 銅器 [5] 鐲子

XXI THE CENTRE

I go there frequently in order to . . .

1 drink a cup of good coffee

2 look at his wonderful pictures

3 practise my Chinese [*or:* French, German, Russian]

4 play the piano [*or:* violin]

5 borrow books

6 read the latest papers and magazines

7 exchange ideas

8 meet friends

9 talk to colleagues about my problems

10 get accurate information

11 inquire about the health of his parents

12 consult the reference books in the reading-room

13 listen to his records

14 listen to the news on the wireless [*or:* see the news on television]

15 to hear her sing

Alternative Headings and/or **Complements:**

XXI

Woo charngx daw nahlii chiuh, wey-de sh . . .

1 he yihbei hao kafei[1]

2 kannx tade heen hao-de huall

3 liannshyi shuo Jongwen [*or:* Fahwen, Derwen, Ehwen]

4 tarn gangchyn[2] [*or* lha hwuchyn[3] (*also:* tyichyn)]

5 jieh shu

6 kann tzueyjinn-de baw her tzarjyh

7 jiauhuann yihjiann

8 kann perngyeou [*also:* yuhjiann perngyeou]

9 her torngshyh-de tarn woode wenntyi

10 derdaw joenchiueh-de shiaushyi

11 wenniv ta fuhmuu-de jiannkang tzeeme yanq

12 tzay yuehlaanshyh char-iv tsankaoshu[4]

13 ting tade lioushengji-piantz

14 ting wushianndiann-de shinwen [*also:* shiaushyi] [*or:* kann diannshyh-shanq de shinwen]

15 ting *ta* chanq gel

Notes: [1] 咖啡 [2] 鋼琴 [3] 胡琴 [4] Cp. p. 13, n. 1.

XXII PLEASURE-SEEKING

I have not . . . for a (very) long time

1 been to the theatre [*or:* cinema] **for a (very) long time**

2 gone for a walk **for a (very) long time**

3 slept all night **for a (very) long time**

4 been to church **for a (very) long time**

5 played the piano **for a (very) long time**

6 played the violin **for a (very) long time**

7 danced **for a (very) long time**

8 done any rowing **for a (very) long time**

9 done any swimming **for a (very) long time**

10 read any novels **for a (very) long time**

11 done any riding **for a (very) long time**

12 gone skating **for a (very) long time**

13 played cards **for a (very) long time**

14 been to a concert **for a (very) long time**

15 talked Chinese **for a (very) long time**

Alternative Headings and/or **Complements**: Cp. Pattern XLIV (*This is the first time I have* . . .).

Woo heen jeou meiyeou . . . le

1 ting shih [*or:* kann diannyiing] le

2 sann buh le

3 shuey yiyeh-de jiaw le

4 daw liibaytarng chiuhle

5 daa gangchyn[1] le

6 lha hwuchyn[1] le

7 tiawwuule

8 yau[2] [*also:* hwa[3]] chwan le

9 fuh[4] shoei le

10 kann sheaushuo le

11 chyi maa le

12 hwa bing le

13 daa pair le

14 ting inyuehhuey le

15 jeang [*also:* shuo] Jonggwohuah le

Notes: [1] See p. 43, n. 2 and 3. [2] 搖 [3] 划 [4] 浮

XXIII THE TEETOTALLER

I never . . . because . . .

1 **I never** drink wine [*or:* beer] **because** it makes me sleepy

2 **I never** go to this restaurant **because** it is too expensive

3 **I never** go by this train **because** it is too crowded

4 **I never** work in the evening **because** I feel too tired

5 **I never** go by this ship **because** it is too slow

6 **I never** tell him any secret **because** he will always tell other people

7 **I never** contradict [*or:* criticise] him **because** he is easily offended

8 **I never** invite him **because** he is too dull

9 **I never** eat with chopsticks **because** I am not used to it

10 **I never** read in bed **because** it is not good for my eyes

11 **I never** go climbing **because** it makes me giddy

12 **I never** smoke **because** it makes me cough

13 **I never** drive quickly **because** it is dangerous

14 **I never** get up early **because** I am too lazy

15 **I never** go back on my words **because** I do not wish to disappoint people

---

Alternative Headings and/or **Complements:**

XXIII

Woo tzoongbu [*also:* laobu] . . . inwey

1 **Woo tzoongbu** he jeou [*or:* pyijeou[1]] **inwey** woo hele yiihow jiow kuenn

2 **Woo tzoongbu** daw jehgeh fanngoan chiuh **inwey** tay guey

3 **Woo tzoongbu** tzuoh jehtsyh huooche **inwey** tay (yeong)jii[2]

4 **Woo tzoongbu** tzay woan-shanq gongtzuoh **inwey** woo jyueder tay ley

5 **Woo tzoongbu** tzuoh jehtyau chwan **inwey** ta tzoou-de tay mann

6 **Woo tzoongbu** gawsuh ta mihmih[3] **inwey** ta yeongyeuan gawsuh byede ren

7 **Woo tzoongbu** faanbor [*or:* pipyng] ta **inwey** ta heen rongyih der tzuey

8 **Woo tzoongbu** chiing ta **inwey** ta tay buh-tsongming

9 **Woo tzoongbu** yong kuaytz chy fann **inwey** woo yonqbuguann

10 **Woo tzoongbu** tzay chwang-shanq kann shu **inwey** nah dueyyu woode yeanjing buh hao

11 **Woo tzoongbu** par shan **inwey** nah jiaw woo yunn

12 **Woo tzoongbu** chou ian **inwey** nah jiaw woo kersow

13 **Woo tzoongbu** kai kuay che **inwey** nah heen weishean

14 **Woo tzoongbu** tzao chii **inwey** woo tay laan

15 **Woo tzoongbu** shy shinn[4] **inwey** woo bwu yuannyih jiaw ren shy wanq

---

Notes: [1] 啤酒 [2] 擁擠 [3] See p. 31, n. 5. [4] 失信

XXIV FLABBERGASTED

I was so frightened that . . .

1 I did not know what to say (could not say a thing)

2 I left at once

3 I even forgot to leave a tip

4 I even forgot to say good-bye

5 I even forgot to thank him

6 I even forgot to light my cigarette

7 I could not go on with my work

8 I remained silent (did not say one word)

9 I dropped the letter

10 I did not even ask him where he was going

11 I did not even ask him to sit down

12 I did not even apologize

13 I made no attempt to resist

14 I suddenly talked to him in my mother tongue [*or:* in English]

15 I did not even ask whom he had married

Alternative Headings and/or **Complements:**

XXIV

Shiah·de . . .

1 woo du shuobushanq huah laile

2 woo lihkeh jiow tzooule

3 woo lian jeouchyan du wanqle geei le

4 woo lian tzayjiann du wanqle shuo le

5 woo lian shieh du wanqle daw[1] le

6 woo lian ianjeual du wanqle dean le

7 woo buh neng tzay wanqshiah tzuoh gong le

8 woo lian yijiuh huah du meiyeou shuo

9 woo baa nahfeng shinn tsorng woo shoou-lii diawshiahchiuh le

10 woo lian (wenn) ta wanq naalii chiuh yee [*also:* du] mei(yeou) wenn

11 woo lian chiing ta tzuohshiah yee mei(yeou) chiing

12 woo lian daw[1] chiann[2] du [*also:* yee] mei(yeou) daw

13 woo du mei(yeou) sheang diikanq

14 woo huran shuochii woode beengwohuah [*or:* Ingwen] laile

15 woo lian ta cheule shwei woo yee mei(yeou) wenn

Notes: [1] 道 [2] 歉

XXV MR MEMORY

I . . . what he . . .

1 I remember very well **what he** said at the end of last year

2 I shall never forget **what he** once told my father

3 I did not quite understand **what he** proposed just now

4 I do not agree with **what he** told us yesterday

5 I do not know **what he** said about you

6 I never heard **what he** did in Paris

7 I cannot tell beforehand **what he** is going to do

8 I shall ask him **what he** taught our students last week

9 I do not believe **what he** told my (elder) sister

10 I do not want to tell my father **what he** told our headmaster

11 I have not seen yet **what he** showed my mother

12 I have not tasted yet **what he** prepared for dinner

Alternative Headings and/or **Complements:** Note that you can combine almost any two parts of the sentences.

XXV

Ta . . . woo . . .

1 **Ta** chiuhnian-dii (suoo) shuo-de huah **woo** jihder heen chingchuu

2 **Ta** yeou yitsyh gawsuh woo fuhchin-de huah woo yeongyeuan buh neng wanqjih

3 **Ta** gangtsair (suoo) tyi-de (shyh) **woo** mei(yeou) wanchyuan doongder [*also:* mingbair]

4 **Ta** tzwotian (suoo) gawsuh woomen-de (huah) **woo** bwu tzanncherng

5 **Ta** (suoo) shuo-de guanyu nii-de huah **woo** buh jydaw

6 **Ta** tzay Bali (suoo) tzuoh-de shyh **woo** tzoong mei(yeou) ting shuo guoh

7 **Ta** suoo sheangyaw tzuoh-de shyh **woo** buhneng shian gawsuh ren

8 **Ta** shanq-shingchyi (suoo) jiau woomen shyuesheng-de gongkeh **woo** yaw wenn ta

9 **Ta** (suoo) gawsuh woo jieex-de shyh [*also:* huah] woo buh shiangshinn

10 **Ta** (suoo) gawsuh woomende shiawjaang de shyh [*also:* huah] woo bwu yuannyih gawsuh woo fuhchin

11 **Ta** (suoo) geei woo muuchin kann-de dongshi woo hair mei(yeou) kannjiann ne

12 **Ta** (suoo) yuhbey-de woanfann-de tsay **woo** hair mei(yeou) charng ne

---

Notes: Note that the position as in English (*woo jihder heen chingchuu ta chiuhnian-dii* (*suoo*) *shuo-de huah*) is possible but less emphatic

XXVI FUTILE REGRET

If only he . . .

1 hadn't spent all the money

2 hadn't gone home late that night

3 hadn't forgotten to give you a cheque

4 hadn't drunk too much

5 hadn't left her

6 did not always criticize people

7 did not always interfere

8 did not always think that he alone **was** right

9 did not always interrupt people

10 did not always make little presents

11 did not always arrive late

12 did not always tell lies

13 did not always speak so softly

14 did not always look down on other people

15 did not always promise more than is in his power

Alternative Headings and/or **Complements:**

XXVI

Yawsh ta . . . yeou dwo hao ua

1 mei(yeou) huawan chyan **yeou dwo hao ua***

2 nahgeh woanshanq [*also:* nah-i yeh] hwei jia meiyeou woan

3 mei(yeou) wanqjih geei nii jypiaw

4 mei(yeou) he tzuey

5 mei(yeou) likai *ta*

6 buh yeongyeuan pipyng ren

7 buh yeongyeuan gansheh[1] ren

8 buh yeongyeuan sheang ta duey [*also:* sheang chwule ta meiyeou ren duey]

9 buh yeongyeuan daa chah[2]

10 buh yeongyeuan geei ren sheau liiwuh

11 buh yeongyeuan (lai) woan

12 buh yeongyeuan sa hoang[3]

13 buh yeongyeuan sheaushengl-de [*also:* dishengl-de] shuo huah

14 buh yeongyeuan chingkann[4] byede ren

15 buh yeongyeuan yinqsheu ren ta buhneng tzuoh-de shyh

Notes: [1] 干涉 [2] 打岔 [3] 撒謊 [4] 輕看

* Add '*yeou dwo hao ua*' also at the end of sentences 2–15.

XXVII ALL THE DIFFERENCE IN THE WORLD

If she had . . . everything would be all right

1 phoned her husband from the station **everything would be all right**

2 apologised to her father **everything would be all right**

3 known that the child was ill [*or:* had just come out of (back from) hospital] **everything would be all right**

4 been nice to him on that evening **everything would be all right**

5 told him about her nationality **everything would be all right**

6 taken a car **everything would be all right**

7 consulted the doctor **everything would be all right**

8 prepared the speech **everything would be all right**

9 not missed the train **everything would be all right**

10 not seen the advertisement in the newspaper **everything would be all right**

11 not left the country **everything would be all right**

12 not sold the house **everything would be all right**

13 not signed the agreement **everything would be all right**

14 not failed in the examination **everything would be all right**

15 not been dismissed **everything would be all right**

Alternative Headings and/or **Complements**: '*If she had . . . this would never have happened.*' (*Jearu ta . . . jiow meiyeou jehjiann shyh*).

XXVII

Jearu TA . . . yichieh shyhchyng jiow du hao le

1. **Jearu** *ta* tzay huoochejann geei *ta* janqfu daale diannhuah **yichieh shyhchyng jiow du hao le**
2. **Jearu** *ta* shianq *ta* fuhchin dawle chiann **yichieh shyhchyng jiow du hao le**
3. **Jearu** *ta* jydawle nahgeh hairtz yeou binq [*or:* gang tsorng iyuann hweilai] **yichieh shyhchyng jiow du hao le**
4. **Jearu** *ta* nahtian woan-shanq day ta heen hao [*also:* heen herchih-de] **yichieh shyhchyng jiow du hao le**
5. **Jearu** *ta* gawsuhle ta *ta*de gwojyi[1] **yichieh shyhchyng jiow du hao le**
6. **Jearu** *ta* guhle yilianq chihche **yichieh shyhchyng jiow du hao le**
7. **Jearu** *ta* wennle [*also:* chiingle] dayfu **yichieh shyhchyng jiow du hao le**
8. **Jearu** *ta* yuhbeyle nahgeh jeangyean **yichieh shyhchyng jiow du hao le**
9. **Jearu** *ta* mei(yeou) wuh che **yichieh shyhchyng jiow du hao le**
10. **Jearu** *ta* mei(yeou) kannjiann baw-shanq-de goanggaw **yichieh shyhchyng jiow du hao le**
11. **Jearu** *ta* mei(yeou) likai gwo **yichieh shyhchyng jiow du hao le**
12. **Jearu** *ta* mei(yeou) may farngtz **yichieh shyhchyng jiow du hao le**
13. **Jearu** *ta* mei(yeou) tzay hertorng-shanq huahya[2] **yichieh shyhchyng jiow du hao le**
14. **Jearu** *ta* kaoshyh mei(yeou) shybay[3], **yichieh shyhchyng jiow du hao le**
15. **Jearu** *ta* mei(yeou) bey cheh jyr[4] **yichieh shyhchyng jiow du hao le**

Notes: [1] 國籍 [2] 畫押 [3] 失敗 [4] See p. 15, n. 1.

XXVIII GRANDMOTHER'S GLASSES

If the spectacles are not on the table in the dining-room . . . must

1 I **must** have left them at the grocer's [*or:* in the hotel, the office, the club]

2 they **must** be in my bag

3 they **must** be under the pillow in my bed

4 they **must** be on the writing-desk in my study

5 they **must** be on the chair in the garden

6 I **must** have lost them on the train [*or:* on the bus, in the car, in the theatre]

7 they **must** have been taken [*or:* stolen, hidden] by somebody

8 they **must** have fallen on the carpet between the two armchairs in the study

9 they **must** be in the wardrobe in the bedroom

10 they **must** be on the top shelf [*or:* second shelf] of my bookcase

11 they **must** be in the drawer of the kitchen table

12 they **must** be upstairs in the small room

13 they **must** be in that shop where I bought the oranges [*or:* bananas]

14 my daughter **must** have taken them by mistake

15 they **must** be on my nose

Alternative Headings and/or **Complements**: Use 'perhaps' (*yeesheu*) instead of 'must' (*yidinq*). Cp. Pattern VII (*But for him . . .*).

XXVIII

Yeanjinqtz yaw bwu tzay fannting-de juotz-shanq . . . yidinq

1 woo **yidinq** lah[1] tzay tzarhuohpuh-lii [*or:* tzay leugoan-lii, gongshyhfarng-lii, jiulehbuh[2]-lii] le

2 jiow **yidinq** tzay woode pyibau-lii ne

3 jiow **yidinq** tzay chwang-shanq jeentou-diishiah ne

4 jiow **yidinq** tzay shufarng-de shieetzyhtair-shanq ne

5 jiow **yidinq** tzay huayuan-liitou-de yiitz-shanq ne

6 woo **yidinq** diou tzay huooche-shanq [*or:* tzay gonggonqchihche-shanq, chihche-shanq, tzay shihyuann-lii] le

7 jiow **yidinq** yeou ren nachiuhle [*or:* toule, tsarngchiilaile]

8 jiow **yidinq** diaw tzay shufarng-lii nah leangbaa dahyiitz-jongjial [*also:* jongjian] dihtaan-shanq le

9 jiow **yidinq** tzay wohshyh-de iguey-lii ne

10 jiow **yidinq** tzay shujiahtz-de tzueyshanq-i tserng [*or:* dihelltserng] ne

11 jiow **yidinq** tzay chwufarng-lii juotz-de choutih-lii ne

12 jiow **yidinq** tzay lou-shanq-de sheau utz-lii ne

13 jiow **yidinq** tzay woo mae jyutz [*or:* shiangjiau] nahgeh puhtz-lii ne

14 jiow **yidinq** sh [*also:* geei] woode neuel baa ta natsuohle

15 jiow **yidinq** tzay woode byitz-shanq ne

Notes: [1] 落 [2] 俱樂部

Note the alternation between **le** and **ne** in accordance with the tense of the English version.

XXIX SAFETY FIRST!

If you are not careful, you will . . .

1 be run over by a car

2 fall from the steps [*or:* chair]

3 be thrown into prison

4 fall into the river [*or:* sea, lake]

5 upset the tea

6 fall out of the window

7 tear the page

8 burn your finger

9 get into trouble

10 get drunk

11 break the chair [*or:* window]

12 spill the ink [*or:* tea; water]

13 go bankrupt

14 catch a cold

15 make him angry

Alternative Headings and/or **Complements**: Cp. Pattern XV (*He almost . . .*). *Ruguoo* or *ruohsh* could be used for *yawsh.*

XXIX

Nii yawsh buh sheaushin, jiow yaw . . .

1 bey che penqle[1] [*also:* yahsyyle[2]]

2 tsorng titz-shanq [*or:* yiitz-shanq] diawshiahlaile

3 tzuoh jianyuh le

4 diaw tzay her-lii [*or:* hae-lii, hwu-lii] le

5 baa charhwu[3] [*also:* charwoan] penqdaole

6 tsorng chuanghuh-shanq diawshiahlaile

7 baa shu syle

8 baa shooujyrtou (geei) shaule

9 yeou mafarn le

10 he tzuey le

11 baa yiitz nonq huay[4] le [*or:* baa chuanghuh nonq suey[4] le]

12 baa mohshoel [*or:* char, shoei] saale

13 poh chaan le

14 jaur liang le

15 ranq (jiaw) ta sheng chih le

Notes: Note the perfective particle at the end of each sentence. [1] 碰了 [2] *yahsyyle,* when fatal accident, see p. 31, n. 3. [3] tea-pot or cup. [4] *huay* 'broken' in general, *suey* implies the idea of fragmentation.

XXX THE PROPHET

In a year's time . . .

1 the economic situation will have changed completely

2 the houses will all be rebuilt

3 there will be no censorship of the press or correspondence

4 we shall go abroad

5 she will come of age

6 I shall leave school [*or:* go to the University]

7 my wife and I shall travel round the world

8 she will be cured

9 the agreement will come to an end

10 I hope to visit my brother in America

11 there will be no shortage of paper [*or:* raw materials]

12 he will have resigned

13 we shall put on weight because we shall be able to eat as many sweets as we like

14 he will take his first examination

15 I must have another suit

Alternative Headings and/or **Complements:** '*Within one year*' =tzay yihnian-*yiiney*

Tzay yihnian yiihow . . .

1 jingjih-chyngkuanq jiow yaw wanchyuan biannle

2 farngtz jiow du yaw tzay gayle

3 jiow meiyeou shinwen her shinnjiann-de jeanchar[1] le

4 woomen jiow yaw chu gwo le

5 ta jiow yaw daw cherngnian-de niansuey le

6 woo jiow yaw bih yeh le [*or:* yaw ruh dahshyue le]

7 woo her woo neyren jiow yaw leushyng chyuan shyhjieh le

8 *ta*de binq jiow yaw jyhhaole

9 chihiue[2] jiow yaw maan ch(y)i le

10 woo shiwanq daw Meeigwo chiuh kann woode shiongdih

11 jyy-de [*or:* yuanliaw-de] chiuefar[3] jiow meiyeou le

12 ta jiow yaw tsyr jyr le

13 woomende tiijonq jiow yaw tzengjiale inwey woomen keeyi sweibiann chy tarng le

14 ta jiow yaw kao dihi tsyh le

15 woo jiow deei tzay tzuoh yihshen ifwu le

Notes: [1] 檢查 [2] 契約 [3] 缺乏
Note the *le* after *yaw*.

XXXI BALANCED JUDGMENT

In any case . . .

1 we must never lose our temper (get angry) [*or:* despair]

2 he can borrow as many books as he likes

3 you must first pay your debts

4 she can eat as much as she wants

5 you cannot but learn Chinese

6 they should not swear [*or:* fight]

7 this is a sacrifice on his part

8 he is the most intelligent of all

9 the book should not be so expensive

10 he will be back at the end of this month

11 he should not have married this terrible woman

12 she ought not have taken her holiday now

13 he ought not have left you before you had completely recovered

14 it was not his fault

15 he should have told her about his nationality long ago

Alternative Headings and/or **Complements**: Cp. Pattern XI (*Even if . . .*).

XXXI

Wuluenn ruher . . .

1 woomen tzoong bwuyaw sheng chih [*or:* shywanq]

2[1] ta shiihuan jieh jiibeen shu jiow nenggow [*also:* keeyii] jieh jiibeen shu

3 nii bihdeei shian hwan jay

4[1] *ta* yaw chy duoshao jiow neng [*also:* keeyii] chy duoshao

5 nii fei[2] shyue Jonggwohuah [*also:* Jongwen] buh kee

6 tamen buh inggai mah ren [*or:* daa jiah]

7 jehsh tade yihjoong shisheng

8 ta bii shwei du tsongming

9 jehbeen shu buh inggai jehme [*also:* nahme] guey

10 jehgeh yueh-dii ta jiow yaw hweilaile

11 ta buh inggai cheule jehgeh keepah-de neuren

12 ta shianntzay buh inggai gaw jiah

13 tzay nii mei(yeou) wanchyuan fuhyuan yiichyan ta buh inggai likai nii

14 jeh bwush tade tsuoh

15 ta tzao jiow inggai gawsuh *ta* tade gwojyi[3] le

Notes: [1] Note that Chinese has no correlatives. [2] Cp. Pattern XLI (*Simply must . . .*). [3] See p. 55, n. 1

XXXII WEIGHED IN THE BALANCE

In my opinion, he is very . . .

1 clever
2 stupid
3 able
4 patient
5 calm
6 modest
7 modern
8 old fashioned
9 serious
10 influential
11 kindhearted
12 nice
13 conceited
14 curious (inquisitive)
15 witty (facetious)
16 jealous
17 honest
18 cunning
19 conscientious
20 irritable

Alternative Headings and/or **Complements**: 'I don't think he is very . . . '' (*woo buh shiangshinn ta heen* . . .). 'How do you know he is very . . .' (*Nii tzeeme jydaw ta heen* . . .). 'People say he is very . . .' (*Yeou ren shuo ta heen* . . .). Cp. Pattern XIX (*His . . . than mine*).

XXXII

Jiuh woo kann, ta heen . . .

1 tsongming

2 benn [*also:* hwutwu (hwudwu)]

3 yeou nenglih

4 yeou nayshinq(l)

5 chernjinq

6 chianshiu

7 shinshyh

8 laoshyh [*also:* jiowshyh]

9 yanjonq

10 yeou shyhlih

11 herchih

12 hao

13 tzyhdah

14 haw chyi

15 hwaji [*also pronounced:* guuji]

16 jyiduh [*also:* jihduh]

17 cherngshyr

18 jeauhwa

19 rennjen

20 yeou pyichih

Notes: 1 聰明 2 笨 3 有能力 4 有耐性兒
5 沉靜 6 謙虛 7 新式 8 老式
9 嚴重 10 有勢力 11 和氣 12 好
13 自大 14 好奇 15 滑稽 16 嫉妒
17 誠實 18 狡猾 19 認真 20 有脾氣

XXXIII DISINTERESTED

It makes no difference to me whether . . .

1 you wear your red or your blue dress (suit)

2 people love or hate me

3 I go by rail or by plane

4 I see a film or a play

5 the window is open or closed

6 I read English or Chinese

7 I sit on the chair or on the bed

8 I have a large or a small room

9 I have a wireless or not

10 you write to him or not

11 you plant flowers or vegetables

12 you study science or philosophy

13 he has his day-off to-day or to-morrow

14 you write or type your letters

15 she sings or plays the piano

Alternative Headings and/or **Complements**: 'It does not make the slightest difference' would be: ***dueyyu woo yiħdeal meiyeou guanshih.*** Cp. also Pattern VIII

XXXIII

. . . dueyyu woo meiyeou guanshih

1 Nii chuan horng ifwu huohsh lan ifwu . . .

2 Renmen ay woo huohsh henn woo . . .

3 Tzuoh huooche huohsh tzuoh feiji . . .

4 Kann diannyiing huohsh ting shih . . .

5 Chuanghuh kaij huohsh guanj . . .

6 Kann Inggwoshu huohsh Jonggwoshu . . .

7 Woo tzuoh tzay yiitz-shanq huohsh chwang-shanq . . .

8 Woode utz dah huohsh sheau . . .

9 Woo yeoumeiv[1] wushianndiann . . .

10 Nii geei ta shieebuv[1] shinn . . .

11 Nii jonq hua huohsh jonq tsay . . .

12 Nii shyue keshyue[2] huohsh jershyue[3] . . .

13 Ta jintian huohsh mingtian fanq jiah . . .

14 Nii shiee huohsh daa niide shinn . . .

15 *Ta* chanq ge huohsh tarn gangchyn[4] . . .

Notes: [1]Note the rendering of 'or not' by ***yeou-meiyeou, shiee-bu-shiee.*** Note also that ***mei*** and ***bu*** and the repeated verb are unstressed and therefore toneless. [2]See p. 25, n. 4. [3]哲學
[4]See p. 43, n. 2.

XXXIV DESPONDENT

It's no use . . .

1 telling him, he won't listen

2 going on with the discussion, you are too tired

3 asking him, he was not there at the time

4 talking to him, he is deaf

5 investing money in this business, it will soon go bankrupt

6 spending money on repairs, this car is well beyond repair

7 trying to borrow a book from him. He never lends anybody anything

8 being kind to him. He will only do it if you force him to

9 applying for this post, the candidate has already been chosen

10 enquiring about his brother, he has neither seen him nor written to him for the last ten years

11 trying to persuade him to accept this post, I have tried time and again

12 calling the doctor; he has already consulted many, and not one of them could help him

---

Alternative Headings and/or **Complements**:

XXXIV

. . . meiyeou yonqchuh . . .

1 Gawsuh ta **meiyeou yonqchuh,** ta buh keen ting

2 Tzay wanqshiah taoluenn **meiyeou yonqchuh,** nii tay leyle[1] [*also:* tay pyifar[2] le]

3 Wenn ta **meiyeou yonqchuh,** nahgeh shyrhow ta mei tzay nahlii

4 Shianq [*also:* duey, gen, her] ta shuo huah **meiyeou yongchuh,** ta sh longtz

5 Wanq jehgeh shengyih-lii tour tzy[3] **meiyeou yonqchuh,** ta kuay yaw poh chaan le

6 Hua chyan shioulii jehlianq chihche **meiyeou yonqchuh,** inwey ta yiijing buh neng shioulii le [*also:* yiijing shioubuleaule]

7 Shianq ta jieh shu **meiyeou yonqchuh,** inwey ta tzoongbu jieh geei ren sherme dongshi

8 Gen ta herchih [*also:* Day ta heen hao] **meiyeou yonqchuh,** nii fei cheangpoh ta, ta buh keen tzuoh jehjiann shyhchyng

9 Sheang tzuoh jehgeh shyh **meiyeou yonqchuh,** inwey tamen yiijing jaodaw ren le

10 Wenn ta ta shiongdih tzeemeyanq **meiyeou yonqchuh,** (jin) shyrnian lai ta mei(yeou) kannjiann ta, yee mei(yeou) geei ta shieeguoh shinn le

11 Chiuann ta tzuoh jehgeh shyh **meiyeou yonqchuh,** woo chiuann ta haojii tsyh le

12 Chiing dayfu **meiyeou yonqchuh,** ta yiijing kannguoh haojiigeh le, meiyeou yigeh neng bangjuh ta

Notes: [1] 累了 [2] 疲乏 [3] 投資

XXXV THE ALIBI

. . . last Monday night at 7 o'clock?

1 To whom did you phone . . .

2 With whom did you dine . . .

3 With whom did you dance . . .

4 To whom did you speak . . .

5 With whom did you go to the theatre . . .

6 For whom did you call the police . . .

7 With whom did you make an appointment . . .

8 With whom did you play cards . . .

9 Whose class did you attend . . .

10 To whom did you send a wire . . .

11 With whom did you have a row . . .

12 With whom did you share the table (at dinner) . . .

13 For whom did you pay the bill . . .

14 For whom did you go to the post office . . .

15 With whom did you go up in the lift . . .

Alternative Headings and/or **Complements**: Add 'Please tell me' (*Chiing gawsuh woo . . .*) or 'Do you still remember?' (*. . . nii hair jihder bwu jihder(le)*). Cp. Pattern XXII (*I have not . . . for a very long time*).

XXXV

Nii shanqliibay-i woan-shanq chidean jong . . .

1 geei shwei daa diannhuah le?

2 her shwei chy woanfann le?

3 torng shwei tiawwuule?

4 shianq [*also:* duey, gen, her] shwei shuo huah le?

5 her [*also:* torng] shwei chiuh kann shih le?

6 tih shwei jiaw jiingchar lai le?

7 her shwei dinq iuehuey le?

8 her shwei daa pair le?

9 shanq shwei-de keh le?

10 geei shwei daa diannbaw le?

11 her shwei daa jiah le?

12 her shwei tzuoh yigeh juotz (chy woanfann) le?

13 tih shwei hwan janq le?

14 tih shwei daw youjenqjyu chiuh le?

15 her shwei tzuoh diannti le?

Notes: *shanqliibay-i* means 'Monday of *last* week', *liibay-i* 'Monday of *this* week'.

XXXVI FRIENDLY WARNING

Next time don't . . .

1 wait for me in my room but in front of the school

2 talk to the teacher but to the headmaster

3 send him to the post office but to the bank

4 sit on the bed but on a chair

5 send him a letter but a telegram

6 drink wine but milk

7 forget to buy tickets beforehand

8 be late. Get up half an hour earlier

9 rely on your memory. Put the name and telephone number down so that I can ring back

10 climb trees with your best trousers on

11 speak before you are spoken to

12 go before you have breakfast

13 criticise before you know the facts

14 pay the bill before you have checked it

15 go to a foreign country before you know the language

Alternative Headings and/or **Complements**: Cp. Pattern XIII (*From now on I shall never . . .*).

XXXVI

Shiahtsyh nii bwuyaw [*also:* bye] . . .

1 tzay woode utz-lii deeng woo, tzay shyueshiaw-chyanmiann deeng woo

2 shianq jiawyuan shuo huah, shianq shiawjaang shuo huah

3 daafa ta daw youjenqjyu chiuh, daafa ta daw ynharng chiuh

4 tzay chwang-shanq tzuoh, nii tzay yiitz-shanq tzuoh [*also:* tzuoh tzay chwang-shanq, tzuoh tzay yiitz-shanq]

5 geei ta shiee yihfeng shinn, geei ta daa yigeh diannbaw

6 he jeou, he niounae

7 wanqjih [*also:* wanqle] shian mae piaw

8 woan. Tzao banngeh jongtou chii

9 kaw niide jihshinq. Baa shinqming her diannhuahhaw chyuan jihshiahlai inwey woo keeyii daahwei diannhuah chiuh

10[1] Shiahtsyh nii chuanj tzueyhao-de kuhtz-de shyrhow bwuyaw [*also:* bye] par shuh

11[1] Shiahtsyh nii tzay meiyeou ren wenn nii yiichyan bwuyaw [*also:* bye] shuo huah

12[1] Shiahtsyh nii tzay mei chy tzaofann yiichyan bwuyaw [*also:* bye] tzoou

13[1] Shiahtsyh nii tzay mei jydaw shyhshyr yiichyan bwuyaw [*also:* bye] pipyng ren

14[1] Shiahtsyh nii tzay mei dueyiv (janq)dantz yiichyan bwuyaw [*also:* bye] geei chyan

15[1] Shiahtsyh nii tzay mei shyue neygwode huah [*also:* waygwohuah] yiichyan bwuyaw [*also:* bye] daw waygwo chiuh

---

Note: [1]Note the inclusion of the 'Heading' on account of the change in the order of words.

XXXVII BEING DIFFICULT

. . . not . . . enough

1 This room is **not** warm **enough**

2 The soup is **not** hot **enough**

3 The house is **not** big **enough**

4 The soles are **not** thick **enough**

5 This lamp is **not** bright **enough**

6 This train is **not** fast **enough**

7 His essay is **not** long **enough**

8 My collar is **not** clean **enough**

9 His voice is **not** loud **enough**

10 This table is **not** long **enough**

11 This kind of paper is **not** thin **enough**

12 The shoe-laces are **not** strong **enough**

13 This knife is **not** sharp **enough**

14 The meat is **not** fresh **enough**

15 The soil is **not** fertile **enough**

Alternative Headings and/or **Complements:** Use 'too' and the opposites, e.g., 'This room is too cold' (*Jehgeh utz tay leeng*), etc.

XXXVII

. . . bwu gow . . .

1 Jehgeh utz **bwu gow** noan·huo

2 Tang **bwu gow** reh

3 Farngtz **bwu gow** dah

4 Shyedii(el) **bwu gow** how

5 Jehjaan deng **bwu gow** lianq

6 Jehtsyh huooche **bwu gow** kuay

7 Tade wenjang **bwu gow** charng

8 Woode liingtz **bwu gow** ganjinq

9 Tade shengin **bwu gow** dah [*also:* gau]

10 Jehjang juotz **bwu gow** charng

11 Jehyanq-de jyy **bwu gow** baur

12 Shyedall **bwu gow** jieshyr[1]

13 Jehbaa dau(l) **bwu gow** kuay

14 Row **bwu gow** shinshian

15 Tuu **bwu gow** feir

Note: [1] 結實

XXXVIII SOME PLATITUDES

Of course, we must always remember that . . .

1 an ideal solution is impossible

2 natural development is better than enforced reform

3 any kind of failure will cause discouragement

4 no attack can attain its objective without loss

5 sometimes right conclusions can be drawn from wrong premises

6 it is better to take risks than to cancel the plan altogether

7 a rash action may endanger the whole project

8 libraries are an all-important factor in education

9 any progress of mankind depends on a clear insight into the conditions of the past and the present

10 each generation must acquaint itself with the works and achievements of the great thinkers of the past

11 for intellectual workers longer working hours are not likely to (do not necessarily) produce better results

12 most difficulties can be overcome by a compromise

Alternative Headings and/or **Complements**: 'we must realise' *woomen yaw mingbair* [also: *leaujiee*]. 'we must never forget' *woomen tzoongbu yaw wanq(jih)*. Cp. Pattern XLV (*Unless . . . cannot*).

XXXVIII

Dangran woomen bihdeei yeongyeuan jihder . . .

1 yigeh wanchyuan maanyih-de jieejyue sh buh-keeneng-de

2 tzyhran-de yeanbiann[1] bii cheangpoh-de gaeger[2] hao

3 wuluenn naa-i joong shybay du linq [*or:* shyy] ren shywanq

4 jinngong[3] bwu show soenshy buh neng dardaw muhdih

5 yeou-de shyrhow you tsuoh-de jeasheh[4] keeyii tueidaw duey-de jyeluenn[5]

6 woomen ninqkee maw shean, yee bwuyaw wanchyuan cheushiau jehgeh jihhuah

7 ruguoo woomen buh sheaushin, jehgeh jihhuah chyuanbuh jiow yeou weishean

8 twushugoan dueyyu jiawyuh-de guanshih bii sherme du jonqyaw

9 renley-de gehjoong jinnbuh chyuan kaw heen chingchuu-de mingbair guohchiuh her shianntzay-de chyngshyng

10 meei-i geh shyrday-de ren bihshiu jydaw guohchiuh dah sysheangjia-de gongtzuoh her cherngji[6]

11 dueyyu yonq naotz tzuoh gong-de ren tzengjia tamende gongtzuoh-jongdean buh yidinq yeou genq hao-de jieeguoo

12 suoo yeou-de kuennnan du keeyii yonq tyauher[7] jieejyue

Notes: [1] 演變 [2] 改革 [3] 進攻 [4] 假設 [5] 結論 [6] 成績 [7] 調和

XXXIX THE LATEST

. . . only two hours ago

1 He phoned me [*or:* sent me a telegram] . . .

2 My brother left for France . . .

3 I received this news . . .

4 They signed the agreement . . .

5 We rented [*or:* sold, bought] this house . . .

6 His wife died [*or:* passed away] . . .

7 He borrowed the money from me . . .

8 Thieves burgled the house . . .

9 The new class started . . .

10 My father talked to him . . .

11 He moved to another place . . .

12 He resigned [*or:* accepted the post] . . .

13 I repaired his car . . .

14 They had another row . . .

15 He was operated upon . . .

Alternative Headings and/or **Complements:** '. . . just two hours ago' (*chiahcheau yeou leanggeh jongtou*), 'exactly two hours ago' (*jeengx yeou leanggeh jongtou*), 'not quite two hours ago' (*hair bwudaw leanggeh jongtou*), 'approximately two hours ago' (*chahbuduo yeou leanggeh jongtou*).

XXXIX

. . . tsair [*also:* jyy, bwuguoh] yeou leanggeh jongtou

1 Ta geei woo daa diannhuah [*or:* daa diannbaw] . . .

2 Woode dihx [*also:* gex] chii shen daw Fahgwo chiuh . . .

3 Woo jiedawle jehgeh shiaushyi . . .

4 Tamen dinqle jehgeh hertorng [*also:* tamen huahya] . . .

5 Woomen tzule [*or:* mayle, maele] jehgeh farngtz . . .

6 Tade furen syyle [*or:* chiuh shyh le] . . .

7 Ta baa jehbii chyan shianq woo jiehchiuh . . .

8 Tzeir jinndaw farngtz-lii . . .

9 Shin ban chii tour . . .

10 Woo fuhchin [*also:* jiayan] her ta tarn [*also:* shuo] huah . . .

11 Ta ban daw byede dihfang chiuh . . .

12 Ta tsyr jyr[1] [*or:* yinqsheule tzuoh jehgeh shyh] . . .

13 Woo baa tade chihche shiouhaole . . .

14 Tamen yow daale yitsyh jiah . . .

15 Isheng yonq shooushuh[2] jyh ta . . .

Notes: [1] See p. 3, n. 4. [2] 

XL NO COMPROMISE!

Rather than . . .

1 submit to those humiliating conditions we shall fight to the last man

2 allow him to go to the cinema I should keep him at home and make him work hard

3 deal with the subject incompletely writing a few unimportant papers he should prepare a solid treatise in a year or two

4 buy anything cheap I would prefer to spend a little more money and buy something that is really good

5 spend the evening in idle gossip I make a point of reading a good novel

6 always ask for little sums I should ask for a yearly grant (to be paid in four instalments)

7 go to the cinema I should see a good play

8 bother him with questions that anybody can answer I should suggest a subject in which he is an expert for general discussion

9 try a dozen subjects at the same time I should concentrate on one

10 make a patched-up (temporary) peace we shall fight on until victory is reached

---

Alternative Headings and/or **Complements:**

XL

. . . ninqkee . . . yee buh [*also:* bwu]

1 Woomen **ningkee** daa daw tzueyhow yigeh ren, **yee buh** jieshow nahshie ruu gwo[1]-de tyaujiann

2 Woo **ningkee** liou ta tzay jia-lii jiaw ta yonq gong niann shu, **yee bwu** jiaw [*also:* ranq] ta kann diannyiing chiuh

3 Ta **ningkee** yonq i-leang-nian-de gongfu chiuh yuhbey yihbeen heen hao-de shu, **yee buh** charng shiee heen doan-de, dueyyu tyimuh buh heen jonqyaw-de wenjang

4 Woo **ningkee** yonq duo-yihdean chyan mae shyrtzay hao-de dongshi, **yee bwu** yaw mae pyanyi-de dongshi

5 Woo **ningkee** tzay woan-shanq jawlih kann yihbeen hao sheaushuol, **yee buh** shiihuan shuo shyanhuah

6 Woo **ningkee** chiingchyou meeinian geei [*also:* jiuan[2]] woo yihpi[3] chyan (fen syhtsyh fuh[4]), **yee bwu** yuannyih charng yaw heen shao-de chyan

7 Woo **ningkee** chiuh kann yihchu[5] hao shih, **yee bwu** chiuh kann diannyiing

8 Woo **ningkee** tyi yigeh ta juanmen yanjiou-de tyimuh dahjia taoluenn, **yee bwu** yuannyih wenn ta yigeh puutong-ren du neng dar-de wenntyi

9 Woo **ningkee** jyijong tzay yigeh tyimuh, **yee bwu** yuannyih torngshyr shyh heen duo-de tyimuh

10 Woomen **ningkee** daa daw tzueyhow shenqlih, **yee bwu** yuannyih shianntzay yeou yigeh lin shyr-de herpyng

---

Notes: [1] 辱國 [2] 捐 [3] 批 [4] 付

[5] See p. 41, n. 2. Note the inversed order of the sentences in Chinese.

XLI NO ALTERNATIVE

. . . simply must . . .

1 You **simply must** have this tooth pulled out

2 We **simply must** pack our cases

3 He **simply must** take this examination

4 She **simply must** engage another servant

5 My father **simply must** buy him a fountain-pen

6 We **simply must** buy tickets for this play

7 You **simply must** change the tyres

8 We **simply must** invite him to dinner

9 I **simply must** meet him one day

10 He **simply must** have a hair-cut to-morrow

11 You **simply must** consult a doctor

12 We **simply must** finish this work

13 He **simply must** go to bed at once

14 The cabinet **simply must** resign

15 He **simply must** be expelled

Alternative Headings and/or **Complements**: Cp. Pattern XLV (*Unless . . . cannot . . .*).

. . . fei . . . buh kee

1 Nii **fei** bar jehgeh ya **buh kee**

2 Woomen **fei** juang shiangtz **buh kee**

3 Ta **fei** kao shyh [*also:* tour kao[1]] **buh kee**

4 *Ta* **fei** tzay guh yigeh diishiahren **buh kee**

5 Woo fuhchin **fei** geei ta mae yihjy tzyhlaishoeibii **buh kee**

6 Woomen **fei** mae jehchu[2] shih-de shihpiaw **buh kee**

7 Nii **fei** huannshanq wayday **buh kee**

8 Woomen **fei** chiing ta chy woanfann **buh kee**

9 Yeou yihtian woo **fei** yuhjiann ta **buh kee**

10 Ta mingtian **fei** lii faa **buh kee**

11 Nii **fei** chiing dayfu **buh kee**

12 Woomen **fei** baa jehjiann gongtzuoh tzuohwan **buh kee**

13 Ta **fei** jehjiow [*also:* lihkeh] shueyjiaw **buh kee**

14 Neyger[3] **fei** tsyr jyr[4] **buh kee**

15 Ta **fei** bey kaichwu **buh kee**

Notes: [1] 投考 [2] See p. 41, n. 2. [3] 內閣 [4] See p. 31, n 4.

XLII ANTI-COMMUNISM

Tell him this is (these are) . . .

1 my father's collar
2 my mother's shoes
3 her parents' books
4 his (elder) brother's shirt
5 her younger brother's rain-coat
6 my (elder) sister's hat
7 his (younger) sister's umbrella
8 his wife's overcoat
9 her husband's necktie
10 Mr. Li's razor
11 Mrs. Wang's comb
12 his son's hair-brush
13 her daughter's hand-bag
14 my grandfather's photo
15 his grandson's passport
16 my granddaughter's gloves
17 his mother-in-law's money
18 her mother-in-law's letter.
19 his father-in-law's shop .
20 her father-in-law's house
21 my uncle's (father's elder brother) rickshaw
22 her aunt's (father's sister) car
23 my nephew's dictionary
24 my niece's room

Alternative Headings and/or **Complements**: Add 'Don't forget' (see Pattern X), or 'How do you know . . . ?' (*Nii tzeemė jydaw . . . ?*).

Gawsuh ta jeh sh . . .

1 woo fuhchin[1]-de liingtz

2 woo muuchin[2]-de shye

3 *ta*(de) fuhmuu-de shu

4 ta gex-de hannshan

5 *ta* dihx[3]-de yeui

6 woo jieex-de mawtz

7 ta meyx-de yeusaan

8 ta furen-de dahi

9 *ta* janqfu-de liingday

10 Lii Shiansheng-de gualean-dau(l)

11 Wang Tayx-de shutz

12 ta erltz-de tourfaashuatz

13 *ta* neuel-de shooutyibau

14 woo tzuufuh-de shianqpian

15 ta suentzyy-de huhjaw

16 woo suenneu-de shooutaw

17 ta yuehmuu-de chyan

18 *ta* porx-de shinn

19 ta yuehfuh-de puhtz

20 *ta* gongx-de farngtz

21 woo borfuh[4]-de yangche

22 *ta* gux[5]-de chihche

23 woo jerl[6]-de (jyrtz-de) tzyhdean

24 woo jyrneu-de utz

Notes: [1] *or:* [instead of *woo fuhchin*] *jiafuh, jiayan.* [2] *or:* [instead of *woo muuchin*] *jiamuu-de.* [3] *or: shiongdih-de, shehdih-de.* [4] 'father's younger brother' *shwufuh;* 'mother's brother' *jiowx.* [5] 'mother's sister' *yi* (*yel*). [6] 'mother's son' *waysheng.*

XLIII THEORY OF SPECIES

This . . . is not . . . but . . .

1 **This** book **is not** a dictionary **but** an encyclopedia

2 **This** lady **is not** his mother **but** his mother-in-law

3 **This** gentleman **is not** the headmaster **but** the French teacher

4 **This** man **is not** a painter **but** a musician

5 **This** old man **is not** a scholar **but** a politician

6 **This** illness **is not** a cold **but** diphtheria

7 **This** doctor **is not** a surgeon **but** a physician

8 **This** building **is not** a museum **but** a library

9 **This** street **is not** Hatamen Street **but** Morison Street

10 **This** metal **is not** iron **but** lead

11 **This** animal **is not** a lion **but** a tiger

12 **This** boy **is not** Chinese **but** Siamese

13 **This** girl **is not** English **but** French

14 **This** man **is not** a customer **but** the manager

15 **This** gentleman **is not** a student **but** a professor

---

Alternative Headings and/or **Complements**: Cp. Pattern X (***Don't forget, this is not . . .***).

XLIII

Jeh . . . bwu sh . . . sh . . .

1 **Jeh**been shu **bwu sh** yihbeen tzyhdean **sh** yihbeen baekechyuanshu[1]

2 **Jeh**wey tayx **bwu sh** tade muuchin **sh** tade yuehmuu

3 **Jeh**wey shiansheng **bwu sh** shiawjaang **sh** Fahwen-jiawyuan

4 **Jeh**geh ren **bwu sh** huahjia **sh** yigeh inyuehjia

5 **Jeh**geh lao tourtz **bwu sh** shyuejee **sh** jenqkeh

6 **Jeh**geh binq **bwu sh** jaur liang **sh** bairhour[2]

7 **Jeh**wey dayfu [*also:* isheng] **bwu sh** wayke **sh** neyke

8 **Jeh**tzuoh jiannjwu **bwu sh** borwuhyuann[3] **sh** twushugoan

9 **Jeh**tyau jie **bwu sh** Hatamen Dahjie **sh** Wangfuujiing-Dahjie

10 **Jeh**geh jinshuu **bwu sh** tiee **sh** chian

11 **Jeh**geh donqwuh **bwu sh** shytz **sh** laohuu

12 **Jeh**geh nanhairtz **bwu sh** Jonggworen **sh** Shianluoren[4]

13 **Jeh**geh neuhairtz **bwu sh** Inggworen **sh** Fahgworen

14 **Jeh**geh ren **bwu sh** guhkeh **sh** jaangguey-de

15 **Jeh**wey shiansheng **bwu sh** yigeh shyuesheng **sh** yiwey jiawshow

---

Notes: Note the classifiers.

[1] See p. 21, n. 1. [2] 白喉 [3] 博物院 [4] 暹邏人

XLIV THE GREENHORN

This is the first time I have . . .

1 eaten in a Chinese restaurant

2 lost my watch

3 put on long trousers

4 spoken Chinese

5 been ill

6 climbed a mountain

7 been in an air raid [*or:* earthquake]

8 broadcast

9 slept all night through

10 been drunk

11 had a bad dream

12 kissed a girl

13 been in a Chinese house

14 read a Chinese novel

15 seen this play

Alternative Headings and/or **Complements:**

XLIV

Jehsh woo dihi tsyh . . .

1 daw Jonggwo-fanngoantz chy fann

2 dioule woode beau

3 chuan charng kuhtz

4 shuo Jonggwohuah

5 yeou binq

6 shanq shan [*also:* par shan]

7 yuhjiann hongjah[1] [*or:* dihjenn]

8 goangboh

9 shueyle yiyeh-de jiaw

10 he tzuey le

11 tzuohle yigeh eh menq

12 her neuren jie woen[2]

13 daw Jonggwo farngtz lai

14 kann(le) Jonggwo-sheaushuo

15 kann [*also:* ting] jey-i chu[3] shih

Notes: [1] 轟炸 [2] 接吻 [3] See p. 41, n. 2.

XLV SINE QUA NON

Unless . . . cannot . . .

1 **Unless** he divorces his wife he **cannot** inherit his father's fortune

2 **Unless** he forgets about the past and altogether changes his behaviour we **cannot** be friends

3 **Unless** this proposal is carried unanimously the rules **cannot** be changed

4 **Unless** he has full confidence in the treatment the doctor **cannot** cure him

5 **Unless** you know the language of a country you **cannot** understand the mind of the people

6 **Unless** everything is prepared down to the last detail we **cannot** succeed

7 **Unless** the student has sufficient time for homework, and frequently revises the material which he has learnt, he **cannot** hope to reach his objective in reasonable time

8 **Unless** strictest secrecy is kept about all his movements we **cannot** carry out our plans

9 **Unless** we adopt new scientific methods we **cannot** raise the present standard of living

10 **Unless** we all co-operate and every one of us does his utmost we **cannot** achieve victory

---

Alternative Headings and/or **Complements**: Cp. Pattern XLI (. . . *simply must*).

XLV

Chwufei . . . buh neng . . .

1 **Chwufei** ta her tade furen lihuen, ta **buh neng** cherngjih[1] [*also:* jihcherng[2]] ta fuhchin-de chyan

2 **Chwufei** ta wanqle guohchiuh-de shyhchyng baa tade shyngwei wanchyuan gaele, woomen **buh neng** tzuoh perngyeou

3 **Chwufei** jehgeh tyiyih[3] neng chyuantii tongguoh, nahshie gueitzer **buh neng** biann

4 **Chwufei** ta wanchyuan shinnyonq jehgeh jyhfaa, dayfu **buh neng** jyhhao ta

5 **Chwufei** nii jydaw yigeh gwojia-de yeuyan nii **buh neng** doongder [*also:* mingbair] tamen renmin-de shinlii

6 **Chwufei** yichieh du heen sheaushin-de heen shyangshih-de yuhbey, woomen **buh neng** chernggong

7 **Chwufei** shyuesheng yeou chongtzwu[4]-de shyrjian yuhbey gongkeh, charngx uenshyi ta yiijing shyueguoh-de tsairliaw, ta **buh neng** shiwanq tzay shiangdang-de shyrhow dardaw tade muhdih

8 **Chwufei** tade shyngdonq neng baoshoou-de heen mihmih[5], woomen jiow **buh neng** shyrshyng woomende jihhuah

9 **Chwufei** woomen yonq shin-de keshyue-fangfaa, woomen **buh neng** tzenggau shianntzay-de shenghwo-cherngduh

10 **Chwufei** woomen dahjia du hertzuoh[6], meei-i geh ren jinn ta tzueydah-de lihlianq[7], woomen **buh neng** derdaw shenqlih[8]

Notes: [1] 承繼 [2] 繼承 [3] 提議 [4] 充足

[5] See p. 31, n. 5. [6] 合作 [7] 力量 [8] 勝利

XLVI FRUSTRATION

When we got there eventually . . .

1 the guests had all gone

2 the bank [*or:* the shop, library] had already closed

3 the workmen had gone on strike

4 the last train had just left

5 the tickets had all been sold

6 the case had been collected by somebody else

7 the furniture had been removed

8 I realised that I had forgotten the key

9 the lecture was over

10 he had already signed the agreement

11 the man was dead

12 the police was waiting outside the door to arrest us

13 the town had already been occupied by the enemy

14 he had already been taken to hospital

15 the cable had been cut

Alternative Headings and/or **Complements**: Cp. Pattern XLVII (*While I was asleep . . .*).

XLVI

Gaandaw [*also:* deengdaw] woomen mohxleaul daw nahlii-de shyrhowl . . .

1 kehren yiijing du [*also:* chyuan] tzooule

2 ynharng [*or:* puhtz, twushugoan] yiijing guan men le

3 gongren yiijing bah gong le

4 tzueyhow-i tsyh che gang kaitzoou

5 piaw du maywanle

6 shiangtz yiijing jiaw [*also:* bey] byeren cheutzooule

7 jiajiuh yiijing nakaile

8 woo tsair jydaw woo wanqle yawshyr le

9 jeangyean yiijing wanle

10 nahgeh hertorng ta yiijing huahyale

11 ren yiijing syyle

12 tzay menkooul yiijing yeou jiingchar deengj na woomen le

13 jeh cherng yiijing jiaw·dyiren jannle

14 tamen yiijing baa ta sonq daw iyuann chiuhle

15 diannshiann yiijing duannle

Notes:

XLVII THE SLEEPING BEAUTY

While I was asleep . . .

1 the fire went out

2 the house caught fire [*or:* collapsed]

3 thieves came and stole all my belongings

4 the children turned the room topsy turvy

5 he ate my dinner

6 she packed her case and left the house quietly

7 the postman threw a letter through the door

8 he emptied the bottle

9 the rain poured through the open window

10 the clock stopped

11 he rushed into the room and woke me up

12 she prepared my tea

13 she polished my shoes, brushed my clothes, and sewed the buttons on

14 she broke my desk open and removed the letters

15 he pawned my gold watch and her pearl necklace

Alternative Headings and/or **Complements:** Cp. Pattern XLVI (*When we got there eventually . . .*).

Woo shueyjiaw-de shyrhow . . .

1 nah huoo miehle

2 farngtz jaur huoo le [*or:* tale[1]]

3 tzeir jinn farngtz laile baa woo suoo yeou-de dongshi du touchiuhle [*also:* nachiuhle]

4 sheau hairtzmen baa utz nonq-de luann-chi-ba-tzau[2] le

5 ta baa woode woanfann chyle

6 *ta* baa *ta*de shiangtz juanghaole, heen anjinq-de likaile jehsuoo farngtz le

7 sonqshinn-de [*or:* youchai] baa yihfeng shinn tsorng menfenq-lii rhengjinnlaile

8 ta baa pyngtz heguangle [*also:* heganjinqle]

9 yeu tsorng kaij-de chuanghuh jinnlaile

10 guahjong tyngjuhle

11 ta paojinn woode utz-lii lai baa woo jeaushiingle[3]

12 *ta* baa char yuhbeyhaole

13 *ta* tsale woode shye, shuale woode ishang, yow ferngshanq neoutz le

14 *ta* baa woo shieetzyhtair-de choutih daakaile baa nahshie feng shinn du natzooule

15 ta baa woode jinbeau her *ta*de jutz-shianqchiuan[4] du danqle

Notes: [1] See p. 7, n. 1. [2] 亂七八糟 [3] 攪醒

[4] 珠子項圈

XLVIII PRIVATE DETECTIVE

Who is the . . .

1 gentleman in the blue suit?

2 old man with a beard?

3 child in the corner sitting on the lady's lap?

4 old woman with the pimple on the nose [*or:* with a goitre]?

5 professor that has just arrived?

6 actor with the foreign accent?

7 student on crutches that arrived late?

8 white-haired guest that came last?

9 last but one visitor?

10 teacher leaning against the wall with a book under his arm?

11 old lady with spectacles standing near the fire?

12 servant with the (wine-)red nose?

13 young man with the straw hat [*or:* felt hat]?

14 young lady in Chinese [*or:* Western] clothes?

15 little boy that is reading a newspaper?

Alternative Headings and/or **Complements:** *Did you see the . . . ?* (*. . . nii kannjiannle meiyeou?*).

XLVIII

. . . sh shwei?

1 Nah chuan lan ifwu-de shiansheng . . .

2 Yeou hwutz-de laotour . . .

3 Tzay nahgeh jeau-lii tzuoh tzay neuren toei-shanq-de sheau hairtz . . .

4 Byitz-shanq jaang ge·da[1] [*or:* bortz-shanq jaang lioutz[2]]-de lao tayx . . .

5 Gang daw-de nahwey jiawshow . . .

6 Yeou waygwo-koouin-de chanq shih-de ren . . .

7 Laiwoan-de [*also:* chyr daw-de] nahgeh jiah goai[3]-de shyue-sheng . . .

8 Mohxleaul lai-de yeou bair tourfaa-de nahwey kehren . . .

9 Dawshuu-dihell lai-de nahwey kehren . . .

10 Kawj chyang, gebey-diishiah jiaj yihbeen shu nahgeh jiawyuan . . .

11 Tzay lutz-parngbian jannj day yeanjinql-de nahwey lao tayx . . .

12 Yeou jeoutzau[4]-byitz nahgeh shiahren . . .

13 Day tsaomaw [*or:* janmaw] nahgeh nianching-de ren . . .

14 Chuan Jonggwo-ifwu [*or:* yang ifwu] nahwey sheaujiee [*also:* neushyh] . . .

15 Kann baw-de nahgeh nanhairtz . . .

Notes: [1] 疙瘩 [2] 瘤子 [3] 架拐

[4] 酒糟

XLIX THERE ARE MORE THINGS IN HEAVEN AND EARTH

Who would have thought that . . .

1 one day the aeroplane would become an ordinary means of communication

2 he would suddenly draw a gun and would threaten to kill me

3 he would be taken prisoner while driving in his car

4 this play would be a success [*or:* failure]

5 he would become such a great man

6 two people so different in temperament and social standing would get married

7 he would not prove worthy of our confidence

8 the government would suddenly be overthrown [*or:* that the cabinet would resign]

9 the enemy would have evacuated this town without a fight

10 this man would die in a foreign country

11 the weather would change so suddenly

12 he would be punished so severely [*or:* sentenced to be hanged, sentenced to be shot]

Alternative Headings and/or **Complements:**

XLIX

Shwei jydaw . . . ne

1 **Shwei jydaw** feiji yeou yihtian yaw biannwei heen puutong-de jiautong-gongjiuh **ne**

2 **Shwei jydaw** ta huran nachu chiang lai hehhu[1] woo yaw daa woo **ne**

3 **Shwei jydaw** tzay ta kai chihche-de shyrhow jiow bey dyiren nachiuh **ne**

4 **Shwei jydaw** jey-i chu[2] shih nenggow cherngong [*or:* shybay] **ne**

5 **Shwei jydaw** ta yaw cherngwei jehme dah-de [*or:* nahme yeou ming-de] ren **ne**

6 **Shwei jydaw** nahleanggeh pyichih her shehhuey-dihwey nahme buhtorng-de ren yaw jie huen **ne**

7 **Shwei jydaw** ta buh jyrder woomen shinnrenn[3] **ne**

8 **Shwei jydaw** jenqfuu huran (yaw) bey tueidao [*or:* neygger huran (yaw) tsyr jyr] **ne**

9 **Shwei jydaw** dyiren meiyeou daajanq jiow baa jehgeh cherng tueychuchiuh **ne**

10 **Shwei jydaw** neygeh ren syy tzay waygwo [*or:* bwu tzay jia syy] **ne**

11 **Shwei jydaw** tianchih huran (yaw) biann **ne**

12 **Shwei jydaw** ta bey cherngfar-de nahme lihhay [*or:* bey pannjyue[4] jeausyy[5], bey pannjyue[4] chiangbih[6]] **ne**

Notes: [1] 嚇唬 [2] See p. 41, n. 2. [3] 信任 [4] 判決 [5] 絞死 [6] 鎗斃

L THE QUITTER

Why did you go without . . .

1 paying the rent?

2 settling your account?

3 leaving some money for me?

4 talking things over with me?

5 asking for your parents' consent?

6 writing [*or:* phoning] to her?

7 asking me for a letter of recommendation?

8 saying goodbye (taking leave)?

9 consulting your doctor [*or:* lawyer]?

10 making the room tidy?

11 apologising to him?

12 booking a room?

13 buying some presents?

14 enquiring about the conditions over there?

15 making a contract?

Alternative Headings and/or **Complements:** Cp. Pattern VI (*Before I . . . I usually . . .*).

Nii wey sherme tzay (mei) . . . yiichyan jiow tzoou ne?

1 geei tzuchyan **yiichyan jiow tzoou ne?**

2 hwan janq **yiichyan jiow tzoou ne?**

3 geei woo liou yihdeal chyan **yiichyan jiow tzoou ne?**

4 her woo taoluenn jehjiann shyh **yiichyan jiow tzoou ne?**

5 derdaw nii fuh(chin) muu(chin)-de yinqsheu **yiichyan jiow tzoou ne?**

6 geei *ta* shiee shinn [*or:* daa diannhuah] **yiichyan jiow tzoou ne?**

7 chiing woo geei nii yihfeng jiehshawshinn **yiichyan jiow tzoou ne?**

8 gaw tsyr **yiichyan jiow tzoou ne?**

9 wenn niide dayfu [*or:* liuhshy[1]] **yiichyan jiow tzoou ne?**

10 baa utz shyr·dwo [*also:* shyr·dou, shyr·de[2]] hao **yiichyan jiow tzoou ne?**

11 shianq ta daw chiann **yiichyan jiow tzoou ne?**

12 dinq utz **yiichyan jiow tzoou ne?**

13 mae jiigeh liiwuh **yiichyan jiow tzoou ne?**

14 daating nahlii-de chyngkuanq **yiichyan jiow tzoou ne?**

15 dinq hertorng **yiichyan jiow tzoou ne?**

Notes: [1] 律師 [2] 拾掇